Please return or renew book
by last date shown above.

south
AYRSHIRE
C O U N C I L

Dedication
This volume is dedicated to Murray:
it's a response to his patient encouragement
as I have laboured in the midst of strenuous forebears.

Clydebuilt

The Story of George Reith

MARISTA LEISHMAN

SAINT ANDREW PRESS

Edinburgh

First published in 2012 by Saint Andrew Press
SAINT ANDREW PRESS
121 George Street
Edinburgh EH2 4YN

ISBN 978-0-7152-0938-7

British Library Cataloguing in Publication Data
A catalogue record for this book is available from the British
Library. It is the publisher's policy to only use papers that are
natural and recyclable and that have been manufactured from
timber grown in renewable, properly managed forests. All of the
manufacturing processes of the papers are expected to conform to
the environmental regulations of the country of origin.

Originated by The Manila Typesetting Company
Printed and bound in the United Kingdom by
CPI Group (UK) Ltd, Croydon

Contents

Contents

Acknowledgements

As a piece of historical fiction, the stories that make up this book arise from verifiable facts. For these, in regard to the range of the developments attached to the River Clyde, I have drawn on the definitive volume by John F. Riddell: *Clyde Navigation: A History of the Development and Deepening of the River Clyde* (John Donald, 1979). I have appreciated both the clarity and the style with which his material, often complex, has been presented. In addition, Professor John Hume has most generously ensured the accuracy of the historical material, with emendations as needed.

To my further advantage, I have in my possession an enclosure volume, in which my father, John Reith of the BBC – George Reith's grandson – carefully preserved letters and documents significant in the life of his esteemed forebear. Since the grandson worked to model himself on his grandfather in many aspects of behaviour and attitude, as well as style in leadership, I have had this further example to which to refer.

From these sources have clearly emerged the principal aspirations and achievements of this Reith of the Clyde in his role as General Manager of the Clyde Navigation Trust. He understood that his priority was to oversee the deepening of the river to a consistently navigable depth from Glasgow Harbour at the Broomielaw to its estuary at Erskine. His

Chief Engineer was encouraged to design ever larger and more effective dredgers. Then came the need to win over the minds of the city councillors to the urgent need to install sewage treatment plants. For this he had to gain the support of his own Board, this endeavour being outwith the remit of the Navigation Trust.

Early on, George Reith despite his grim demeanour knew how to encourage young entrepreneurs. The Navigation Trust would, promised, also back the design and installation of the most colossal quay-side cranes. And he could communicate readily with the workforce – superiority was not his mode. The teamwork spirit boosted both morale and output.

George took delight in the opening of the new ship-building yards on the river banks. On his initial visit to Glasgow he went to visit the Mavisbank yard. By the end of his tenure, the Trust saw to the commercial development of the city through the opening up of extensive docks and wharves.

Both of the generations of these Reiths, George and John, came from modest social backgrounds. They enjoyed a capacity to get alongside the workforce, on whose loyalty, hard work and, indeed, endurance in the toughest of working conditions ambitious schemes depended. Worldly wise, they well knew that this understanding with the workforce must never bypass the need to build up trust, and to consult with management, at every point.

George Reith was at home with balance sheets; he was careful to ensure that every new enterprise was expertly costed, with decisions resting on the viability of the project. It came naturally to him to scotch many a proposal aimed at the glorification of the Trust, rather than its central purpose in support of the development of the river for shipbuilding, heavy engineering and commerce. Thus it was that the conspicuous building that eventually housed the Trust had to wait until after his retirement and death.

As a young man George Reith grew up in rural Kincardineshire, serving an apprenticeship in his uncle's business as wheelwright. Again, I have been able to enjoy the gentle scholarship of Professor Alexander Fenton in his *Scottish Country Life* (Tuckwell Press, 1999). From this source it has been possible for me to contextualize much of George Reith's work as a wheelwright, as well as to gain impressions of the attitudes and skills of his immediate relatives in this work context.

I have appreciated the courtesy and professionalism of the staff of the Mitchell Library.

As a writer, discovering that you are losing your eyesight, you search around for some wreckage to which to cling. But for me it was not wreckage but a lifeboat that sailed in to the rescue. Frances Hendron coasted smoothly into the turbulent waters of my experience and prepared my concluding chapters to a publisher-ready condition. Also on board that lifeboat was Michella Samy whose patience, precise thinking and experience enabled me to keep cool and clear in the midst of my many-coloured hieroglyphics, pointers and textual replacements. To all this Michella applied rapid computerized technology, so that I received back my work as so many perfected printouts. This support system has been consistently backed up by Steve and Kirsty, our son-in-law and daughter, who, despite their office already heaving under its workload, never delayed in updating me with every message, in whatever form it arrived. I warmly appreciate the readiness with which their help has always been offered.

Of course I have from time to time experienced the task as impossible. To which comes back a most robust response from the family; remember you're 80!

Foreword

This book by Marista Leishman tells the story of a man, a river and a city at a time of transition.

The man is George Reith, her great-grandfather. She paints a vivid picture of him as a driven authoritarian, 'feared rather than loved', but respected as someone who got things done.

When he was appointed General Manager of the Clyde Navigation Trust in 1864, the river was silted, sluggish, smelly and in places little more than a stream. By the time he retired in 1889 it had been transformed into a vast industrial waterway, lined with massive cranes, wharves, docks and the world's leading engineering workshops and shipyards. These improvements helped make Glasgow the Second City of the Empire.

Despite her advancing years – she is now in her eighties, with failing eyesight – Marista sets out to answer two questions. How was the industrial revolution on the Clyde accomplished? And what impelled George Reith to do what he did?

The middle years of the nineteenth century were times of rapid change, when nothing seemed impossible for engineers. Steam took over from sail, iron replaced wood in ships' hulls, the paddle gave way to the screw propeller. New inventions destined for world markets meant that Glasgow was producing far more than the Clyde could accommodate.

Reith set about dredging the river, promoting its purification and providing space for industry along its banks. He commissioned the Princes Dock, the largest facility of its kind in the world at the time. He encouraged the shipbuilders who over the next century were to send 25,000 liners, battleships, ferries, dredgers, tugs and yachts out to sea – all of the highest 'Clydebuilt' standards.

He negotiated his way through the challenges of getting agreement from councillors, parliamentarians, industrialists and local lords who objected to their rural idyll being changed. And when things went wrong, such as the loss of over a hundred lives when the *Daphne* capsized at its launch at Stephens Linthouse in 1883, Reith was quickly there both to comfort the bereaved and to assure the business classes that progress could not be stopped.

Marista seeks to give her readers a sense of the galaxy of progressive talent in Scotland at the time. She introduces into her tale a series of fictionalized meetings between Reith and some of them : the engineers Thomas Telford and Robert Stevenson; the pioneers of the ocean-going steamers, David Napier, Charles Randolph, Robert Napier and Sam Cunard; the reforming Lord Provost of Glasgow, Robert Stewart, who brought clean water to the city from Loch Katrine; the mathematical physicist, genius and professor at Glasgow University, Lord Kelvin; and, because no understanding of the Reith family would be possible without reference to God, the theologian and leader of the 1843 Disruption, Thomas Chalmers.

In seeking to answer her own question about where Reith's drive came from, Marista writes that he believed 'the hand of the Almighty was upon him to accomplish some great task for the public good'. It was a sentiment shared by her own father John Reith, the first Director General of the BBC.

The family's Free Kirk Presbyterianism was rooted in rural Kincardineshire. The Reiths, she writes, were as 'prickly and tenacious as the wild gorse' on the hillsides of home. They introduced the heavy horse to their farm, and damn those who said otherwise. They opposed the local laird and his claims to nominate their minister. They were firm in their belief in church democracy, equality of opportunity for all and the freedom of every man to speak direct to his Maker. And even though both of George's parents succumbed to drink, they still saw one son become a lawyer – who in turn was able to secure a management job for his brother in Scotland's North Eastern Railway, which provided the training and skills for his subsequent career on the Clyde.

The values of hard work, careful control of money and the need for Principles in seeking a greater End served Scots Presbyterians well as they climbed the British ladder. But there was a downside too – an unwavering belief in their own rectitude, the 'belittling of women' (as the author recalls from her own experience), and the winning of respect rather than affection from others.

Clydebuilt, therefore, turns out to be more than the story of the industrialization of a river.

Marista is descended from George's second son, who became a minister of the Free Kirk (almost an exculpation, she suggests, for his father not ascending into the pulpit himself). Her own father was shaped in that same faith. He carefully annotated his grandfather's papers in his own hand, in spidery red ink. And, during his long years at the BBC, he always had a portrait of him on his office wall.

'Is it not curious,' she asks, 'that my father was sufficiently unsure of his identity to need to search out and adopt that of another?'

This book, then, is more than the story of a man, a river and a city. It is also a journey of personal discovery. It is satisfying that Marista, now in her eightieth year, can now conclude that she will never again have any doubts about where her own roots reside.

GEORGE REID
The Rt Hon Sir George Reid

1

The Camlachie Burn

Two men made their way down a track which closely accompanied a tumbling burn. A family resemblance suggested father and son, aged 45 or so and 15. The tension that was building up between them was obvious. The younger of the two, whose legs were long and whose brow was furrowed with frustration, would have preferred his own company. Tall for his age, the boy had strong facial features and a resolute look.

'This Camlachie burn, Father,' said he, 'what is the point of keeping on following it down? This is boring!'

The complaint of the disgruntled teenager almost never yields a satisfactory and conclusive response; but this time the father's happy attempt proved to be oddly accurate, as he tried to assure his son that something of interest would soon appear. He spoke more in hope than knowledge. Just then, however, sounds of an industrial process hard at work were unmistakable. Alexander, the third Reith of that name, felt himself vindicated and rather lucky. His next remark, however, lacked that fine tuning called for in relation to the young. 'There you are, George. You go on ahead and tell me what is happening.'

George, however, true to the spirit of teenage rebellion, stuck to his place behind his father on the track. The two of them plodded on in silence.

As they rounded a clump of hazel, large letters painted across the length of a blackened industrial building appeared: 'Camlachie Foundry'. But it was not, after all, the foundry that compelled their attention. It was the surprising antics of a full-grown man apparently playing with model boats in the burn. He seemed not to notice the bystanders, so absorbed was he in his activity. Certainly, he was working as though with an objective in mind. He had erected a tripod across the burn; it supported a wooden barrel, over which were slung some cords that he used to control the movements of his model boats in the water below. Every now and then, he would stretch out, grab a model that was making heavy weather of the current and mutter to himself impatiently, as he threw it onto the grass beside him.

George, in respectful silence, planted himself as near the activity as politeness would allow. From the bank on which he now sat he realized that, far from play, some form of practical research was in progress: the model boats were being arranged in an order of sorts. At their head was a boat shaped like a walnut shell; its prow was rounded. Next to it lay one of a similar shape but less plump. The progression of the line demonstrated that those shapes, as they neared the end, were increasingly streamlined. The last in the series had a bow shape that was deeply concave – almost, thought this observant lad, to the point of exaggeration.

Now the stranger with the model ships turned to his audience. Clearly he had been aware of their presence but delayed interrupting his task. With hand outstretched to the older of the two he said, 'I'm David Napier, I design ships.'

George Reith listened closely: shipbuilding on the Clyde – how could this be? Even at 15, George knew that the river was too shallow and silted up for that to be worthwhile. Clearly this man with his ships' models was looking to the future.

'The yard that I work with my father is at Camlachie, the next village downstream,' Napier added.

'Well,' said the older of the onlookers, 'we hope you'll excuse our pausing to watch. I'm Alexander – Alexander Reith, and this is my son George. We're here on a visit, from the north-east, from Stonehaven. I'm the keeper of the toll-house there.'

But George, tiring of these niceties, spoke away: 'I've been guessing that you are experimenting with the different forms that you have carved in order to find out which shape copes best with the oncoming waves. I noticed,' he went on, encouraged by the reception that he was getting, 'that your early, very round models were doing much less well than the later. In fact, the farther along the line you worked them the better they performed. Could you try the last one in the line? How would she do, do you think?'

'You're a smart lad!' said the approving marine engineer. 'I'm full of hopes that that design will work for a large ocean-going passenger ship. Here, George! Would you attach this line for me?' He handed the boy a tiny screw and twine and instructed him what to do. Then off shot Napier to collect his father and a colleague. He was a man clearly at the height of his powers and energy.

With the onlookers now swelled to four, David Napier put the last trial model gently into the stream. With a little coaxing from the twine that he held, she positioned herself into the oncoming waves. To his delight, and the congratulations of the onlookers, she held steady, riding the waters.

'Well!' said David, as carefully he drew his precious model out of the stream. 'She's the one of the future! Thanks, George,' he said, turning to the now richly compensated bystander. And the men clapped, and doffed their caps to some great ship of the future, then melted away. The young George Reith, flushed with excitement, turned to his father in the expectation that here was an experience to be shared at last.

They resumed their walk down towards the River Clyde, George delaying as they passed David Napier's Camlachie engineering yard, as he tried to see in as much as possible. Alexander Reith, however, to his son's impatience, appeared to be completely unmoved by the morning's events.

George, deeply impressionable, carried on with beating heart. 'Funny,' he said to himself, 'how some things seem to matter a lot.' Indeed, this random experience was to turn out to be of a marked significance in the career that eventually opened up for this youngster.

One hundred years on, I found myself, aged seven, a passenger on board the great liner herself, the *Queen Mary*. There I was, at the quayside in Southampton, looking up with awe at that great black concave bow: a design, I was later to learn, that had its origins in Glasgow's Camlachie Burn. Now the giant letters of her name; *Queen Mary*, seemed almost to be falling out of the sky onto my head. I saw how the white decks rose in cliffs above me. Most importantly, I was experiencing *her*: I met this greatest of all the ships of the Clyde not as another 'it', like an electric stove or a car, but as 'she', a ship, a living thing, endowed with a creaturely significance of her own. This excitement bore signs of a recognition of sorts. Those three great funnels, black topped and scarlet below, were the livery of the pioneer of shipbuilding and design on the Clyde: David Napier, cousin of Robert Napier. Noble they were as, with huge and stately lean, the tunnels continued gently smoking away.

As we put to sea my father was repeating facts to himself which were apparently of no small significance: 'Clydebuilt,' he said, 'John Brown's: number 534, launched in 1934.'

'Indeed, sir, and what a launch that was from that yard on the north bank.' This was a senior officer speaking: he happened to pass by as the former Director General of the BBC was reminiscing to himself, expressing his own proprietorial interest in the Clyde. The officer, however, was now interrupted by the ship's siren, a sound as from long ago, to make the airwaves tremble.

When that noble din quietened, the officer introduced himself to my father: 'I was a banker until recently, sir,' he said, 'and I managed the account at John Brown's yard for ship number 534.' He had been one of the thousands present at her momentous launch. The emotion of it all had in no way diminished with the passing of time. For three long years No. 534 had stayed no more than a colossal rusting hulk, inert on the stocks in that north bank yard. Cunard could not pay for her completion; her launch, when eventually it was to take place, seemed miraculous.

The officer explained that 'John Brown's' had been founded by two Thomson brothers, local boys. They had worked out of the school of Robert Napier, the man who, along with George Reith, had been behind the ringing title: 'Clydebuilt'. The officer had queued for hours to be at her launch from that Clydebank yard. 'It was carried out by Her Majesty. There was Her Majesty, Queen Mary, ready to speak her piece – a little hesitantly, if I may say so. Then we heard the many hammers that knocked the wooden chocks out of place, all that remained to hold her. Inch by inch the great hulk started to move – would she stick? We held our breath. Then the drag chains, which were in place to control the rush to the river, began to fling themselves about like things possessed. The great ship was moving now, plunging towards the river, we worried that she was going too fast. The crowd scarcely breathed. Then – there came a roar of applause and every cap was raised as she slid into the murky water.'

Obviously reliving the emotion of the occasion, he described tug boats closing in on her as though in an attack of sorts: bow hawsers were already connected; at her stern the tugs nuzzled her round against the encroaching shallows. She was, after all, now in a channel only as wide as half her length. So engrossed had they all been in watching the tugs, that they hardly noticed a sudden commotion on the opposite shore. Here, beside the White Cart Water, the crowds gathered to make the most of an excellent vantage point. Now, however, they had to turn and flee the river bank, pursued by a fearful tidal wave, brought about, of course, by the impact of the great hull as it hit the water at last. Each and every one was wearing their round metal badge carrying the number 534, their passport to this view point of the newly named *Queen Mary*.

Meanwhile, beneath, on the north shore, there were all the tugs, tearing about with excited siren blasts and short black plumes of smoke like punctuation marks. All in the greatest contrast to the shifting of that slow majestic hulk. Thirty thousand tons of steel travelling to the water, and now quietly at rest. Every possible accident had hung like a thunder cloud over the head of the yard manager, he in his bowler hat and alone on his special platform. Supposing she hit the water in a terrible rush, with insurmountable problems following? But no, gently she had gathered speed. Checked by all those drag chains, the great ship was moving on. Too fast? How could she possibly fit into what appeared to all those onlookers as no more than a shallow point? No one breathed. Then, like a man stunned by a mighty blow the yard manager began unsteadily to climb down from his solitary platform, he and his bowler hat.

Suddenly, like a clap of thunder, there had come a mighty roar from the crowd. Every cap and bowler hat had been raised. People struggled to hide their tears. Lightly, it seemed, and all unsurprised, *Queen Mary* now rode the waters of that murky pond into which, daringly, she had been let loose. Though she stuck on the Dalmuir bend, eventually tide and tugs and the terrible thrust of those mighty engines shifted her, and she surged into the first of her Atlantic crossings.

George Reith's grandson was visibly moved by the well-told tale. So great, indeed, was the appeal of this man's story that this hyper-critical audience was for once entirely accepting of the cheerful jumble of events that had tumbled out for his especially attentive ear. Even though *Queen Mary* had been launched well after George Reith's leadership of the Clyde Navigation Trust, here was now lively testimony to his prime drive to make the river navigable and so to energize the swelling scene on Clydeside: that of a river at last able to accommodate the most colossal launch event.

George Reith's vision had ultimately resulted in 40 ship-building yards, numerous docking facilities, both wet and dry, and the warehouses of Glasgow, made now, as never before, within reach of the Atlantic.

Our senior officer recalled, with some difficulty, the task on which several minutes before he had been engaged, and now, a little embarrassed, heard the assurance that his narrative had been of the greatest interest. In those days 400,000 tons of shipping a year had been launched from the Clyde; and 'Clydebuilt' was recognized world-wide. I wondered if it was only huge *Queen Marys* that were 'Clydebuilt'. Later I was to learn that there were innumerable battleships, tankers, dredgers, cruisers and yachts, as well as liners. In Glasgow there came to be an aristocracy of iron and steel, as well as of the men who worked them.

Years later, our daughter Martha, with compelling exactitude, bought tickets for us for an enactment of Bill Bryden's play *The Shipbuilders*. There we were peering down from high tiered seating into the life-size skeleton of a ship under construction. The theatre was the vast former Harland and Wolff shed. In due course our 'ship' slid down the way and into the water.

But George Blake was to write in *Down to the Sea* (Collins, 1937) how great a change had taken place:

Now the Clyde is very different. It was, in a sense, a succession that he witnessed, the high tragic pattern of the Clyde. Yard after yard passed by, the berths empty, the grass growing about the sinking keel blocks. He remembered how, in the brave days, there would be scores of ships ready for launching along this reach . . . and how the men at work on them on high stagings would turn from the job and tug off their caps and cheer the new ship setting out to sea. And now, only the gaunt dumb poles and groups of men, workless, watching in silence the mocking passage of the vessel . . . It was a tragedy beyond economics . . . it was that a tradition, a skill, a glory, a passion, was visibly in decay and all the inherited and acquired loveliness of artistry was rotting along the banks of the stream.

Portrait of Marista Leishman, 1969

2

The First Alexander Reith

George Reith's forebears were tenant farmers, mostly in the vicinity of Stonehaven on the Scottish north-east coast. The first of whom we know worked high on the hill above the old Slug Road out of Stonehaven to Banchory (Slug, appropriately here, is Gaelic for gorge or ravine.) He was Alexander Reith, and was George Reith's great-grandfather. Born in 1708, 100 years before George, he was the first of three of that name. He worked the holding at Clachanshiels, a land of high moorland on the south side of the road. It was undrained, unenclosed, and treeless. Up here, Alexander Reith leaned into the gale – and introduced the heavy horse to replace oxen as the power source for his work. His desire to innovate passed down the line to his great-grandson but, in both cases, it had to be innovation on their own terms, and not on anyone else's. For the grandson the appropriate mode was newly designed dredgers for Glasgow's silted-up river. For Alexander Reith, despite the unpromising nature of his land that brought in a meagre return, the crops were planted apparently on any and every patch of land that might yield. It is likely that Alexander had heard of 'the Improvers'; but he certainly wasn't going to be bothered with them; still less, told by them what to do.

The Improvers were men of some standing in the community as landowners; the best of them wished to bring their influence to bear on agricultural methods. They encouraged innovation in land management and the cultivation of crops with a view to improving yields; to introduce, where possible, adaptable machinery, replacing inefficient and cumbersome contraptions. And – especially testing – they encouraged local people to accept the benefits from discarding old methods in favour of changing ways and new habits.

These benign modernizing initiatives did not accord well with such a combustible character as Alexander Reith, since he felt that any change worth its name could only originate with him. With word reaching him from time to time of inno-vations in draining, fertilizing with lime, clearing, and manur-ing, old Reith would keep to his well-tried ways. 'Improving' also meant fencing off areas, often by building stone dykes, in order first to subdivide the land for specific purposes, like grazing or crop bearing, and secondly to replace the old idea of land held in common by neighbouring farmers, a system which couldn't but result in certain fallings out among neigh-bours and consequent neglect.

Alexander, however, continued with the 'lazy bed', or *fean-nag*, technique: a series of raised beds with ditches in-between, tilled by hand with a spade. The word 'lazy' in no sense referred to the exertions called for but rather to the unculti-vated strip in - between each bed.

The traditions in which the first Alexander's forebears had worked the land were bred in him as immovably as the boul-ders that lay stubbornly across it. 'No, no,' said he, glaring at interfering enquirers, 'I do things my way. Those boulders have been there since we wis wrapped in ice; they're bedded in by now, an sae am I. They leave me alone: I'll do the same for them.' Reith's identification of himself with the chill obstinacy of the scattered boulders was apt. Despite the oddity of his logic with its religious overtones, his neighbours on Toddie

Brae and at Snob Cottage felt themselves dismissed, and went on, among themselves, to decide that that settled the matter. Someone's idea of Reith taking on the running of the local farming commune was a ridiculous one. He was the kind of man, after all, who felt that, for no fault of his own, everyone owed him a living, and that the world had let him down. 'What a thrawn wretch he was,' they said.

Lastly, there was that matter on which no decision had yet been taken: the case of old Flora Macdonald, brought up at Tentyhillock. She had left 45 years ago in order to earn in the coal mines of Coatbridge, and was now looking to return to her native heath. In those days, the 1760s, it was by no means unknown for women and children to work in the Scottish mines. They were seen to be more amenable to carrying coal from the hewing face to the pit bottom, and then up spiral stairs to the surface. It was no wonder that the local community, among whom Flora had grown up, felt keenly their responsibility to care for her in her well-earned retirement.

The tradition in such cases had always been that the local community would build a modest dwelling for those of their number, who, in their old age, were seeking to return to their home patch: a single room with box bed and cast-iron stove would be provided. And, between them they undertook the responsibility of seeing to her welfare. 'An' what did I hear our friend Reith say about old Flora, eh? She was coming back to sponge on the rest o' us.' In their way the Reiths held to their gritty beliefs and attitudes, applying them across the lands and parishes in as prickly and tenacious a way as the wild gorse, or whin, that tightened its grip on every hillside and valley.

Alexander Reith's patient wife, Maggie, had learned to expect a meagre helping of affection and consideration. He felt her advice, as a mere woman, would be of little worth. It was odd that, unaware, Maggie would support her husband in his view. From their different perspectives they both understood the roles of men and women as they were seen at the time by the rising class of industrialists in the cities, and now increasingly in the rural areas. In this view the head of the household was an awful personage who sat in a special chair, used by no one else, at the head of the table at the fireside, with his hat on his head; often to be served meals from special dishes of which no one else, not even guests, and certainly not the women in the family, would eat. In all the arrangements of the household his convenience and wishes were primarily studied, he himself approached only with care and deference.

The older Alexander Reith's view of things was totally entrenched. He had in the meantime made up his mind to replace his team of four oxen, which had dragged the 'old Scotch plough', as it was called, with two Clydesdale horses, on the grounds that the heavy horse had already won himself a reputation for being more powerful and more amenable than oxen. He certainly didn't discuss his risky idea with Maggie.

Into this regime, Alexander automatically fitted his eldest son, also Alexander, assuming that he, as his son, would be naturally equipped with leadership capacities and the ability to command respect. He was unconcerned that the young Alexander had largely copied his father's irascibility and tendency to pick quarrels, out of little or no provocation; the son would try on his father's aptitude for belittling the other, but, in his case, without a shred of authority. The second Alexander would be left looking silly.

Father and son, in their quest for a pair of Clydesdales, took the stagecoach from Stonehaven to Edinburgh. It was spring 1757 and in Edinburgh, having warmed themselves up in a pub in Candlemaker Row and found beds for the night there, the next day they attended the stallion show of Clydesdales in the Grassmarket, close by. That was the important market for this new breed from Lanarkshire. Conscious of the risk that he was taking, Alexander senior made his selection and had the pair that he had bought shipped from Leith to Stonehaven, from where he and his son walked them to the high farm of Clachanshiels.

In sour mood, after a troublesome journey, they fetched up at last at Clachanshiels. The horses needed, somewhat against their will, to be groomed, after which they were fed. Young Alexander was sent chasing around to find the one bag of oats that they had, and which they must supplement with straw – poor in food value for such large and strenuous beasts. Then the pair were turned out. Finding grass at last beneath their feet sent them off in thunderous joy, cavorting around their field, from time to time neighing hugely and then pausing to snatch at some grass. After a bit they settled down to graze, still disturbed at the loss of their familiar companions and by the journey.

Eventually, the men had succeeded in harnessing the pair to the plough, but by this time a crowd of onlookers was gathering for the treat, already uttering catcalls and jokes. They came from Bossholes and Tentyhillock with the idea of criticizing – although they couldn't help admiring, in spite of themselves. The two beasts were magnificent to see, their bay coats gleaming in the early morning autumn sunshine. The men come to see the sight stood languidly at their ease, some of them with their hands thrust deep into their pockets, the smoke from their pipes drifting lazily into the air above them, and giving it a sharp sweet tang. Others hooked their thumbs into their waistcoats, an unmistakable signal that they were there in the role of spectators only, scepticism warring with curiosity. Others still stood by with their arms folded across their chests, a sure indication in the body language of men of the north-east that they were disassociating themselves from what was about to happen. This hiding of hands – in pockets, in weskits, in the folds of their flannel sarks, or shirts – conveyed a powerful message to the Reith men: they were on their own. The expectant huddle there that day was in no mood for revelation; all they wanted was that their inbuilt disdain for experiment would be vindicated by those horses; they would not live up to the promise invested in them by the anxious owners.

Failure was perilously close. 'Hey, Alexander!' called out one mocking voice. 'Maybe ye should try some corrierieuchin [cosy chat] – with the beasts, mind, an' see if ye can all agree about what ye're doing! If they had a tongue in them as foul as your own they would be giving you the rough edge o't by now, they just canna make head nor tail o' what ye're on about.' That a certain truth was being spoken here was something that did little to sweeten Alexander's temper and his embarrassment at that moment. 'Anyway,' went on the same persistent voice, 'I'm away now to get on with some *real* wark . . . you comin wie's, lads?' And several peeled off from among the circle, sighing and exclaiming as they went.

'Yon's a daft sheme, yon,' they judged. 'How much did he pay, our friend Reith, think ye, for yon two?'

'What'll he feed them on? Straw and corn? Not nearly enough! They'll get through a lot more than the oxen, sure as death.'

On they went, their unwelcome voices becoming fainter as they disappeared down the hill; the air remaining heavy still, with their scepticism and their amusement.

Meantime, questions were arising as to why it was, after all these years, that old Clachanshiels was at last clearing the land of boulders, which seemed to be one of the first tasks for the horses. And, even more strange, it had been observed that he was dragging the hefty stones into his stack yard as though for some set purpose, heaping them up in the corner. He was not, as might have been expected, using them to build stone dykes – that new and very practical idea, by which his black cattle would be enclosed, so that his wheat and oats could grow unmolested where they had been sown. Clearly he had some other purpose, which he was not explaining to anyone, not even to his family.

Consistent perhaps with his nature, and with admirable courage, the first Alexander Reith persisted with his scheme. He became the ancestor his great-grandson George Reith of the Clyde was not wholly ashamed of, recognizing, as he was bound to do, that some of his characteristics had been handed down the line. And so, six months on, the neighbours who still turned up to watch him at work with the two Clydesdales, now named Moses and Aaron, found an effective team working not only to turn the soil, but to drag away the delaying boulders.

'The hivvy horse,' he said to anyone who thought to argue with him, 'is the way things are going. Just look at them two.' Alexander turned in admiration towards his own great pair, now placidly at work on their nose bags, the soothing sound of their munching usefully calming their volatile master, as from time to time a massive hoof clattered onto the cobbles and a docked tail flicked against the tormenting flies.

It's true that there was a little of 'I'll show them' in Alexander's next move. Among all the encouraging messages that reached him there had been some that brought news of neighbouring farmers who were introducing horses. The ribaldry which had greeted Alexander's bold move was starting to be replaced by supporting arguments, all of which were brightened up by slender experience. The matter was discussed with vehemence, mostly in several of the 40 houses licensed for the sale of liquor which were to be found in the moderately sized Stonehaven and described by the stridently pious voices of the evangelical wing of the church as 'too many' and as 'dens of iniquity'. The voices critical of Alexander were already starting to lose their force as horses replaced oxen. Alexander, however, relished the zest that attached itself to the ongoing controversy, being shrewd enough to appreciate that the more vigorous the debate the more support it gathered for his ideas. He would make of his premises a centre for horse shoeing, preparing a part of his yard for the purpose, with walls to house a smithy and forge. After all, the nearest smiddy was to be found only in Stonehaven, ten miles away, itself a hindrance to the development of this new power source in agriculture.

And so, one change begat another. Without even an Improver to bend over him and advise – nay, direct – Alexander Reith was introducing a change in farming methods, here in northeast Scotland, which was to last 200 years, until the coming of the Titan tractor in the 1920s. But he would never see himself as allied with the Improvers.

Alexander's daughter, Mariota, was expected to accustom herself to the introduction of the horses in her own way. The men saw her role as being to make herself useful to them – insofar, that is, as was possible. Still unfamiliar with the pair, she found herself one day urgently required by her brother to hold them both while he went off to collect equipment. Without a word of explanation he thrust the reins at her.

'What do I do if they start tae move off?' she said anxiously.

'Dinna let them,' was the unhelpful reply.

'But how do I do that?'

She was told to stand in-between them, and if they started to move – 'which they winna' – to copy Alexander, who now, in an unnecessary show of strength, jerked the reins, in turn startling the pair so that they threw up their heads and backed away. 'That's all there is to it,' said he, and moved off importantly.

Mariota looked up, as on either side of her these high and hillocky beasts rose up into the blue sky above. An instinct told her that one way to get in touch with them, and to avoid trying to control them, where she would surely lose, would be to talk to them and stroke them. Quickly came the peaceful response: from first one and then the other there heaved a huge sigh. Mariota was delighted – the heads dropped lower; one began a comfortable grinding of his teeth, setting his bit to rattling; with them both eyelids started to close and ears drooped to the side. This peaceful scene was broken up when Alexander came back, to grab the reins and call out noisily to them to 'Get on' – and to 'MOVE'! Mariota was sad as she watched them being led away, by now with much tossing of heads and side-stepping. She had started to experience something of that natural affinity which runs deep between people and beasts – especially on the land – and to feel that understanding rather than the strident imposition of will was the way to win trust and obedience. For herself, she again experienced the urge to start a new life: marriage would be the answer.

3

From Wagons to Railways

Young George Reith, Alexander's great-grandson, had worked during his teens in his uncle's wood yard at Kirkton of Durris, near Aberdeen, learning the wheelwright's skills. While he worked steadily and faithfully the impression of the young David Napier at work testing his ship models for seaworthiness on the Camlachie Burn was seldom far from his thoughts. At last – and two years after he had become a married man – he earned himself leave, and, avoiding his uncle's curiosity as to his intent, he arranged to meet his brother David, a young lawyer in the firm of Messrs Adam and Anderson in Aberdeen. He might, he thought, find his way into railways through the firm's involvement with them in the north-east.

George, who was now 36, had of course been in Aberdeen before; but now it was as though he were arriving for the first time. Having booked his seat on the Deeside to Aberdeen coach, he found that the passage was not a simple case of sitting back and enjoying the countryside. Regulations for passengers had been drawn up to ensure that the many long hills along the way might be tackled more effectively. That is, passage was on condition that all passengers accepted the active part that they must play to relieve the exertions of the sweating horses, and to ensure the safe completion of the journey. And so, George stood at the side of the road, and as the coach approached he thought what a brave sight it made, drawn by four powerful Percheron horses. Quickly he found his place, on top among the cheapest seats of the fully loaded coach. A little later, with the horses already bathed in sweat, they halted at the foot of a long brae. The guard jumped down and announced the terms of the travel arrangement: 'First class passengers sit still; second class passengers come oot and walk; third class passengers get doon and shove!' George, naturally in the last category, leaned into his task with vigour.

At last at the Aberdeen terminus, George set out on foot to find his brother's office. But the size and grandeur of the buildings, the bustle of the horse-drawn traffic and the throng of the people, disconcerted him. He felt his confidence and his purpose draining away as he walked. He stopped to peer into a shop window, not so much because he was interested in the wooden furniture which it sold but in order to gather his wits and decide what to do next.

George remembered his first visit to his brother some years before. On that occasion he had thought to find a kindly citizen and seek directions for his brother's address, where he worked as a young advocate. He pulled a crumpled piece of paper out of his pocket on which was written a number in Market Street. 'It's near the harbour,' David had told him.

David was three years George's junior; yet, here he was, nicely set up with a substantial training and earning capacity to match; while he, George, was still fumbling about in his uncle's wood-turning yard. He tried to temper his frustrations as he approached an elderly man walking towards him: he had, he noticed, a kindly look about him. George stepped up and asked him if he could help him find the way.

George remembered how he had been aware that first time, that his appearance lent him an unflattering distinction. Not one to give the slightest thought to how he looked, he had noticed that others were more tidily dressed then he. He had, after all, fled the wood yard still with a certain amount of wood shavings and sawdust clinging to his coarse grey shirt, or sarge, and to his crumpled trousers. Come what may, having negotiated his leave with the greatest care, he had to achieve his objective, which was to be in time to take his third-class place in the Deeside to Aberdeen coach.

The kindly citizen, who was looking up at him with friendly amusement, agreed that Market Street very nearly bordered the harbour. He further offered to accompany him, though hesitating at George's expression to ask if he would be happy with that and not too bored by his company. George remembered he had gladly accepted the offer. As he walked the same route again, he relived the earlier encounter. The white-haired gentleman had paused, to reach and dust off some wood shavings from the young man's left shoulder. 'Here,' he thought to himself,' is a young person with a presence that he doesn't yet quite understand, trying to find his direction in life.' He sighed heavily. Throughout a long and varied life he had developed a fine skill in detecting promise and application in young aspirants to his trade. Here, in this bewildered young giant, he sensed, in raw form, the very qualities for which he regularly searched but didn't always find.

Meanwhile, George was moving on from his feelings of insecurity attaching to his experience of the bustling city, the more constructively now to engage in this new exchange. As the conversation had flowed, he found himself appreciating in the stranger a sense of a life lived in strenuous endeavour; in risk and innovation; in moving with quiet conviction in circles where a new idea was not a bad thing, just because it was new. The stranger's tales again and again revealed his view that patient negotiation must be maintained with those who held controlling reins of power, but who had no more than a diminished grasp of possibilities creatively extended. This old man, with signs of a once powerful physique, tempered by the diminishing effects of old age, seemed to carry his own distinction, qualified by modesty. A man who walked in the company of a thronging past of his own – a man, to George's mounting embarrassment, still unidentified.

His difficulty was compounded when a passer-by, catching sight of the old man, stopped abruptly, bowed to him very formally, and at the same time swept off his bonnet in grave salute.

'Ah,' said George's companion, more to himself than to George, 'one of the town council here in Aberdeen, I think. He also had something to do with the Craigellachie project, I do believe.'

This remark came as a merciful beacon to young George. 'Craigellachie?' cried he, in larger tones than he had quite intended. 'Not the bridge . . . the iron bridge? Are you . . . ?' Here words failed him.

'Thomas Telford is my name,' returned the other, in quiet helpfulness.

'Sir! . . . ' said George – and then stopped short, in a great confusion. Some passers-by were turning round to look curiously at the pair.

But the older man was covering over for the younger. 'I'm pleased to meet you,' he said with deep courtesy, at once directing attention away from himself. 'But I must ask your name, if you please.'

George spoke his name distinctly, and added that he was an apprentice wheelwright, working in his uncle's yard at Kirkton of Durris.

'Ah,' said the other, 'now you are rightly looking to develop your practical skills and to specialize. But tell me, before we go into that exciting field: how are they getting on with the new bridge at Banchory? You see' – he muttered confidentially – 'I have always suspected that they are building that bridge with insufficient clearance for a flooded river. Because,' he said, in a new rush of amicability, 'you and I know what the Dee can get up to in bad weather. In other words, I don't think those piers are tall enough to carry the bridge clear of flood water. I wonder if that might be your view too?'

George thought carefully before replying; but he realized that he could truthfully acknowledge that a similar thought had struck him. Thomas Telford allowed himself to be questioned as to his achievements by the eager young man, recognizing that this was an exchange that might just be of some help to young George as he weighed up his options – residing, as they might, somewhere between the law and engineering.

And so, as they walked amiably along side by side, George entered keenly into Mr Telford's luminous past and achievements, about which he had worked to keep himself informed: those hundreds of miles of roads; his Parliamentary churches, all so neat and chaste, deftly in tune with their rural surrounds – as too were his accompanying manses, each with its own becoming diffidence. Then came the moment when George felt that he could return to this man's most colourful achievements. In particular he had seen etchings of that iron miracle: the Craigellachie Bridge in Banffshire. Here Mr Telford had been working on an especially bold innovation.

'Did you draw on the assembled experience of the Ironbridge Gorge in Shropshire?'

'Ah,' said Mr Telford, in warm response, 'if I had to guess where you might one day be working, it would be in the field to which I lay humble claim. You won't,' he continued modestly, 'have by any chance been to Wales and seen my bridge over the Menai Straits? More ironwork, and oh my, what a site! Even more daunting was my first sight of the gorge formed by the Water of Leith in Edinburgh and with that the commission to bridge it. The Dean Bridge, they called it on its opening day. It was to connect Edinburgh's brave New Towns with its latest initiative, this time another New Town with even more grand houses across the river. And, my, how they argued and delayed on that one. I thought I would never get the go-ahead – not, that is, until I was too old to carry it out. But – in due course the commission arrived on my desk; and then it was me, wondering whether this time, what with all their dithering, I could manage so daunting a task.'

As his narrative touched on the personal, George noticed how his speech softened into the musical lilt of the Scottish Borders. Yes – he remembered Mr Telford's father had been a shepherd in Dumfriesshire; his learning had been at the local school. George was silent as he digested this further achievement against the background of its nurturing. A thought which struck home as he realized, not for the first time, that he himself frequently struggled with the scarcely articulated difficulty that he would be denying his own background – nay, scorning it even – as he reached out to levels of skill and responsibility hitherto unrealized in his own family. How well he knew that such topics did not go down well at home.

George could never have known of a certain very great man who, working in America was an exact contemporary of his. This was Ralph Waldo Emerson, a philosopher and theologian who worked out of his home town of Concord, Massachusetts. His essay 'Self Reliance', in which he soliloquized on the problems attaching to self-realization and discovery, dealt precisely with the position in which George now found himself. George, however, had a mind that would have been well up to the task of tackling this unfamiliar mode of thought and expression, and would have engaged with the new horizons offered by this thinker:

23

A man should learn to detect and watch that gleam of light which flashes across his mind from within, more than the lustre of bards and sages. Yet he dismisses without notice his thought, because it is his. In every work of genius we recognise our own rejected thoughts: they come back to us with a certain alienated majesty . . . 'Trust thyself': every heart vibrates to that iron string . . . Great men have always done so and confessed themselves childlike to the genius of their age, betraying their perception that the absolutely trustworthy was seated at their heart.

But at home George had struggled to grow up and out so that he might find himself in a culture of a different sort. 'Aye,' George had one day overheard his father remark to his mother, 'there's young George at it agin; reaching away above himself.' 'And,' said his mother,'just as David is doing. We should just leave them be,' she added sagaciously, sensing that her man was about to produce a pile of objections to the aspirations of their youngest children. 'Whit's no for them'll pass them by and they'll have to make the best of it.'

Now George was trying to come back to this brilliant present. 'Did you ever work in Glasgow?' George remembered enquiring of Mr Telford.

'Well – yes; - a little, on one of their bridges across the Clyde. But there they had a most admirable Superintendent of the River Clyde; a Mr James Spreull, as I recall. All I did was to recommend some modifications to the excellent work done by John Golborne, whereby the force of the tidal activity of the river might be harnessed to act on itself to scour the river bed and carry the silt out to sea, thus preventing it from so regularly becoming clogged with its own mud and getting in the way of a massive development in shipbuilding and commerce. Huge questions they were for the city fathers, with all those wealthy tobacco merchants criticizing and urging them on, desperate to make even more money. But the excellent Mr Spreull was there ahead of me; he knew what to do. I undertook some similar work here, in this harbour. But why the Clyde?' said he, suddenly wheeling round to confront George. 'You have a special interest in the River Clyde?'

George, nonplussed, acknowledged that this might be so; but, he mumbled, really he didn't know why. Except that from what little he knew there seemed to be colossal opportunity in Glasgow, the city now growing up on both banks of the river – an opportunity not just for Glasgow but for Scotland itself. He finished off speaking with great warmth, surprising himself with the surge of feeling that accompanied his not very clear thoughts. 'I would like,' he heard himself say, 'one day to be in the midst of all of that.'

'Well, good for you,' said Mr Telford.

By then they were at David Reith's door. In the general whirl of his mind George noticed that substantial door and brightly polished knocker. Gravely he had turned to Mr Telford; much moved, he had held out his hand in salute, adding that Mr Telford could not know what an honour it had been for George to have met him that day. It was, he added, trying not to sound too rompous, something he would never forget. As he knocked he had turned to watch Mr Telford move away; an old man, but well supported by the lusty struts of his achievements.

Mr Telford too had turned round on a sudden impulse, waved, and called out, 'The very best of luck, George. One day you'll find yourself where you want to be.' George then 22, would have been even more moved had he known that the next year, 1834, would be Mr. Telford's last.

Now, year later, the door was being opened by a servant; again a surprise for the 36-year-old George whose simple thinking led him to expect David on the other side of it. 'Sir?' enquired the servant.

'I'm here to see my brother, David Reith,' said George gruffly, trying to manage his impatience with this – to him – silly show of position. In a moment in swept his brother, conveying, as he did so, an impression of a great pressure of work from which he had momentarily detached himself, and which might, on the instant, compel him to revisit. George, however, had a fearsome feeling that now he was making a terrible mistake; he was surely expecting too much of himself to suppose that he could, without loss of dignity, submit to his younger brother's supervision as he tried to assist him in his work as an advocate. This bumptious young man, who had always done well at his studies and whose undoubted talent had never fitted into the family scene, presented himself now with altered speech, its rough edges chiselled away. George thought his dress dandified – short dark jacket and pale-coloured breeches. 'Very becoming, no doubt,' he said sourly to himself. Now, to make matters worse, he was rushing on to enquire after the family. To George this was further confirmation that he was seen as the stay-at-home, all up to date with the latest domestic happenings. From such an impression he detached himself in weighty manner: no; he was last at home two months ago; and no, he wasn't up to date with the current problems at the tollhouse. Except, he thought to himself, that of the drink he suspected invaded both his father's and his mother's well-being. That, however, was not for sharing just now.

George was to work in his brother's office for some years, familiarizing himself with law and accountancy, until one day there was a knock at the door. In came the servant. 'Mr Reith, sir,' he said, 'beg pardon for intruding but this was handed in from Messrs Adam and Anderson. I was to tell you, sir, that it was urgent.'

'Ah, thank you, Peter,' said David.

Excusing himself for a moment, David scanned the document. 'Well,' said he, 'we are in luck. Our partners across the road from us here – Adam and Anderson – are turning to us to give them the technical support they will need in a railway application they are about to make . . . ' but he left his sentence unfinished to interrupt himself. 'You are interested in railways, George' he said, all the while working hard on several ideas at once.

Never one to allow himself to be taken by surprise, George neither denied nor affirmed the thought, and waited for further development.

David picked up where he had left off. 'Just now, as you may well know, too many small companies are trying to make a go of connecting centres in Angus and the Mearns one with another, opening up lines almost at random, working incontinently and without strategic thought of any kind. With the result that any profits they may make are swallowed up hopelessly fighting one another, trying for buy-outs and acquisitions, without the least thought as to the public good or the well-being of their own staff. And, would you believe it, they can't even agree among themselves as to the use of a single preferred gauge. Instead, each goes according to his preference, with the result that at the smallest junctions there has to be a whole lot of shunting, which is heavy on time and fuel and dangerous as well. One small mistake on the part of a signalman . . . Now, as if in the face of all this, Adam and Anderson are considering the framing of a bill to cover the stretch from Aberdeen to Forfar and the formation of a company for that purpose. We' – here George noticed the use of the first person plural and felt vaguely stirred in response – 'are invited to join them in this undertaking.'

George said: 'How likely are we to make the same mistakes? Or are you assuming that we will avoid them all?'

Wisely ignoring this, David continued as though talking to himself. 'There will be much more to it than the planning of the route of the line and the decision as to the correct gauge to be adopted. The company will need considerable purchasing powers: locomotives, carriages for passengers, first, second and third class, wagons for moving farm produce around, and now we will need to design and build the so-called "Parliamentary Carriages".'

'Oh?' said George, willing to be enlightened.

Ever ready to oblige, David responded: 'Ah yes! Quite new, it is. In 1845, the Board of Trade, as a result of an Act introduced by James Ewart Gladstone, ensured that railway companies provided cheap third-class travel, especially among the "stopping trains", thus enabling working folk to move around to their jobs with ease. The companies were to submit drawings for their designs' – and here David went to a chest of drawers and drew out a series of scale drawings which he explained as having been submitted by the Arbroath and Forfar railway. 'Each coach,' said he, 'must take a total of 30, seated on benches around the sides. After all, we are well beyond the coal belt – the Caledonian Railway Company deals with all of that. For us enlarged stations at both Aberdeen and Forfar would be needed . . . My word! And here am I, already feeling work overload.

'The idea here, I gather,' said he, reading on, 'is to connect the two companies serving Aberdeen, one of which is called the Circumbendibus Company' – he said this with a trace of a smile, but only such as might accord with his neat attire – 'with a new Scottish North Eastern Railway. That might well mean cutting through the city's prestigious residential areas, incurring storms from well-to-do residents in Rosemount and Queens Cross. Parliamentary powers would undoubtedly be called for . . . ' He spoke with relish at this point. 'You'll need to excuse me while I reply to our friends across the way.'

'How are you replying?' said George, with understandable curiosity.

'Why, Yes, of course,' said David. 'Especially as you are on board to swell our numbers.'

Keen to move on from the leisurely pace and meagre outlook as directed by Uncle John, George's tendency when he first worked with his brother was to carefully weigh up arguments and come to a considered judgement. This had been precipitously swept to one side. He had learned to forgo the prudence of his accustomed approach; now he came to think of things from a new angle whereby possibly he had delayed his own progress by failing to recognize opportunities as they occurred. He might now be looking one in the face. Yes, of course, he would go along with events as they were opening out before him.

'All right?' said David. 'I will be answering in the affirmative; Peter will take my reply across soonest.

'Michty me,' said George.

4

George Reith and the Grand Trunk Railway of Canada

Naturally, the conditions under which the two Reith brothers were attempting to work together had their tensions. The younger of the two, David, was qualified in the law and was now introducing his older brother, George, to its processes. This was with particular reference to the legal framework in which North Eastern Railways might be systematized. George, to his gratification, found himself taking on increasing responsibility for the formation of the new Scottish North Eastern Railway. It was, indeed, a generous opportunity which opened up for him. George was already 36 when he joined his brother in 1847. He was impatient with himself for not, so far, having got out and away from his uncle's wood yard. Now he threw himself wholeheartedly into the formation of the new railway company. This, under his lead, emerged from the Eastern Aberdeen Railway. It was the new Scottish North Eastern Railway. They made him Secretary and Managing Director. For eleven years, he and his brother worked out of the same office. George was (almost) happy.

Having been taken on by the firm of Adam and Anderson, Solicitors, for an apprenticeship in the law, he could enjoy this extension to his field of competence. And so, when

George opened a letter from Mr George Blackwell, which was a possible invitation to join the directorate of the Grand Trunk Railway of Canada – there were two qualifying words attached to the job title which he failed to read. Did he, in some sense, block out the words '*of Traffic*' which followed the title 'Managing Director'? These were important words. Had George read them, he would have been clear that the job he was being offered was not that of Managing Director of the enterprise as a whole, but as pertaining to a particular department within the company – Traffic.

When George opened the letter from this Mr George Blackwell, who described himself as Managing Director of the Grand Trunk Railway of Canada, he was by now, so to speak, already programmed to be unable to read what was written before him, so set was he in his beliefs that he could only understand the top post in any concern as appropriate for him to occupy. But, his brother David, on George's invitation, read the letter out loud and drew his attention to the wording '*of Traffic*'.

Anyone thinking sensibly about these matters would have considered that if Mr Blackwell was resigning his position as Managing Director he would have made clear that what he had in mind was the possibility of handing over to Mr Reith. But his letter was brief and casual to the point of carelessness. As was later to appear, this Mr Blackwell was an engineer, at which he may well have excelled; but the far-seeing, strenuous and demanding tasks and attitudes attaching to management were clearly not his to exercise. While he operated out of a limited vision, his addressee did so out of one that was hugely and happily inflated. These two men were never going to understand, or indeed tolerate, one another.

At this point one could question from where these insistent intimations of destiny in George Reith might have come. The life of the child growing up in the tollhouse at Invercarron, out of Stonehaven, had been cramped, noisy and overpopulated with demanding children. For very numbers they lacked attention. Their anxious parents saw themselves as the victims of circumstance rather than recognizing their need to provide aspirations. The children partially understood that drink, to which both Alexander and Mary succumbed, only added to the difficulties.

These were influences from which their youngest children, George, David and Archie, aspired to escape. The three left the land and the claustrophobic world of the Tollhouse, and went into the professions. In angry reaction to the circumscribed life that was doled out to him, George determined that no such conditions were going to limit opportunities within his reach. Nevertheless there were certain intimations of capacities that he had which fed into his volatile and at times explosive nature. These inspirations – for such they were – had come to him through chance encounters with an earlier generation of leading figures, especially those in the then early science of civil engineering: distinguished people who, in the young man's impressionable mind, assumed heroic status. Thomas Telford was one of these, from the encounter with whom more of significance happened to George than being able to find his way to Market Street.

Earlier, and briefly, he had met Robert Stevenson, another figure whom George had made it his business to find out about. He was the man behind the insistent presence of the Bell Rock Lighthouse, whose high, graceful form was occasionally to be seen from Stonehaven itself on a clear day. There it was, 11 miles out to sea, a silent sentinel warning mariners off that vicious underwater reef, the Bell or Inchcape Rock. It stood as ample testimony to Stevenson's tenacity. For George the Bell Rock Lighthouse stood firm as a monument to his aspirations.

The name of Robert Stevenson was already becoming to some extent known locally in Stonehaven as being also that of the brains behind the great Glenury Viaduct, even though its construction had been handed on to another. Of the great engineer Stevenson and his maritime exploits no one could have written more graphically than his own grandson, Robert Louis:

The seas into which his labours carried the young engineer were still scarce charted, the coasts still dark; his way onshore was often far beyond the convenience of any road; the isles in which he must sojourn were still partly savage. He must toss much in boats, he must often adventure on horseback by dubious bridle tracks through unfrequented wildernesses; he must sometimes plant his lighthouse in the very camp of wreckers; and he was continually forced to the vicissitudes of outdoor life.

Since George Reith was one of Robert Stevenson's most devoted admirers, he had looked forward to a major event – the visit by the great man to Stonehaven to see for himself the nature of the hindrance to its prosperity that lay at the centre of its ill-designed harbour. This was the notorious rock, named Craig na Cair, so placed as to block several potential berths for herring boats. Word of a visit of inspection had got around, and the harbour was already ringed with eager spectators keen to witness the engineer's visit. It was, of course, a reconnaissance visit only, but this did not dim the hopes of many that in this might lie a better livelihood for the majority. The accommodation for three herring boats only would be extended to about 16. George Reith, then in his

33

fifteenth year in 1826, was as eager as any to catch sight of Robert Stevenson.

When he arrived Stevenson was escorted by excited members of the local council, his presence often lost among them since he was a small man. At last the leading councillor indicated that he wished to make a general statement. People crowded round, and the councillor made a deft little speech of appreciation of Mr Stevenson's visit and interest in possibly carrying out the work of blasting the rock and redesigning the piers. Loud clapping followed; but like much of the speech it was blown out to sea. Mr Stevenson smiled broadly and bowed to those around. As the posse began to move away to another perspective of the rock and the harbour layout, George saw his chance and inserted himself into the group, never heeding the irritable looks of the councillors busy appropriating Mr Stevenson as theirs. They were quite unable to tolerate an intervention of any kind. But George Reith had paid careful attention to another of Stevenson's plans, one for building a number of new lighthouses.

Now, undismayed, he reached out his hand in greeting and stumbled through his excitement at the opportunity to speak about the prospect of a light on Skerryvore, off the Island of Tiree. 'And . . . and . . . ' – he was working to recall the names of the projected lights which he had rehearsed – 'Dhu Heartach . . . '

This was one of that 'great black brotherhood of the Torran Rocks', as Robert Louis, poet son of Tom Stevenson, chief engineer for this hazardous project, was to write retrospectively. In 1826, the year in which the Stonehaven project was finally realized, these epoch-making projects were scarcely on the drawing board, but they nevertheless generated their own stories.

Then George stumbled out his further recollection of Muckle Flugga, to be built on that last piece of land between Shetland and the Arctic Circle. Embarrassed, he now fell silent; but the smiling engineer, regarding the young man with friendly appreciation, was modest enough to accept the words of his admirer, commenting that he would be handing on these challenges to his sons; there was more work than he could personally undertake, and the next generation should take on some of it.

Here, thought George, he was looking meaningfully at him; his look was penetrating, a twinkle not far from the weather-beaten face. 'Ah, but the Inchcape Rock! That's yours!' said George, vaguely associating its completion with the year of his own birth, 1811. The great man smiled and bowed his acknowledgement. As he moved on George noticed, in the firmness of his step, that of someone more accustomed than many to retaining his grip on seaweed-covered rocks and marshy ground. Some councillors were struggling with their impatience at the interruption by this young man from nowhere. Who did he think he was, for goodness sake!

Encounters like those with Stevenson and Napier continued to figure in George's outlook; unawares, he modelled himself with accuracy on these two towering figures of his age and on others who attracted his notice and in whom he recognized decision-making and transformation, at the same time connecting in himself an urge to innovate, invent and modernize.

Thus now, in his solicitors' office at Adam and Anderson, and not long after they had met in London, on 15 October 1858, George wrote to Mr Blackwell, making cordial reference to their recent meeting, and going on to confirm in writing that 'the terms then suggested are those under which I would agree to undertake the duties of General Manager in Canada of the Grand Trunk Railway . . . '

In the next paragraph he states the salary agreed was to be £1,500 sterling, with commissions in addition. But his grandson, John Reith of the BBC, who had assembled all the significant papers attaching to the career of his esteemed grandfather (now in my possession), notes, in tiny red ink scratches, that this letter is 'GR accepting the General Managership, of the GTR of Canada'. For John the only appropriate position, for either his grandfather George or indeed for himself, was that of Managing Director, no matter what the concern. Oddly enough, exactly like his forebear, John failed to pick up on the significant omission of the key words 'of traffic'.

In much the same way as the grandfather had modelled himself on certain estimable figures, so John Reith, the grandson, grew to imitate his distinguished forebear. Both of these Reith men might readily be found at the centre of a fight: pugnacious characters, they ruled through aggression. George Reith wrote of the duties which 'I understand to be what usually devolve upon the General Manager of a railway in this country . . . ' If George Blackwell did not at this point pick up on this terminology, did no one else? The signs of a company in dispute with itself are already evident; but George Reith's enlargement in the same letter of managerial themes was not noticed by the dazzled Mr Blackwell.

Meanwhile, despite the unclarities and the worries of George's wife Jean, whom he had married in 1834 and who would come to figure hugely in George's career, the Locomotive Department of the Scottish North Eastern Railway gave him a tremendous send-off with a 'testimonial dinner' at the White Hart Hotel in Arbroath on 20 December 1858. The Scottish North Eastern Railway Company Minutes made abundant note of the part played by Mr Reith in the development of the company and its present 'comparative prosperity'. As they noted carefully: 'Mr Reith, having resigned his situation as Secretary and General Manager on securing the position of General Manager of the Grand Trunk Railway of Canada, the Directors cannot accept his resignation without embodying in their minutes a record of the sense they entertain of Mr Reith's services.'

The Board went on to dine with him again on 3 March 1859, and George finally embarked for Canada, immediately on arrival starting work on the terms that he – alone – recognized. Later that year, matters had fallen apart. When a man like this has so evidently no respect for superiors or colleagues, the time for his resignation is approaching – either that or their termination of his contract, or as much of it as has been accepted by both sides.

George's grandson John Reith succeeded brilliantly in impersonating his grandfather – to the extent that many of the descriptions of the earlier Reith, as well as of his attitudes and capacities, came to apply with uncanny exactitude to the Reith two generations on. Both Reith men, George and John, speedily raised themselves to positions of influence and trust. George was one of the first in Scotland to foresee the prosperous future of railway enterprise in the country, and qualified himself to take a leading part in its direction. He was a man of affairs, quick to grasp principle and intricate details of business; he held very positive opinions, and in matters of controversy held his ground with dogged resolution. For him, the slightest compromise with wrong on grounds of expediency amounted to the bedrock of despicable cowardice. It was rightly said of him that his piety was the austere discipline of the Puritan and the Covenanter. He was a fighting man all his days. With this disposition he was admirably fitted for work in which difficulty and opposition had to be met and overcome. He was a man of unbending integrity and obstinate rectitude. For both men the way to deal with the future was to invent it: the one with railways and the

37

shipbuilding industry; the other with broadcasting and the harnessing of the power of the ether.

But now, in Canada, George was being asked to resign; this he refused to do, unless by special arrangement. Naturally George had more to say on the subject of the reasons for the trouble. He wrote:

> I should have had full powers to carry out my own policy in conducting the Company's approach. On any other footing I should not have accepted the appointment nor in any way connected myself with what I believed had been a grossly mismanaged concern.
>
> In short: . . . that another gentleman with the title of Managing Director was to hold the title which I had gone out to fulfil, and that mine was to be a subordinate one . . . No-one who knows me could suppose that I would countenance such a course of procedure and none who know the inevitable corruptions that prevail among persons in places and power in Canada and the transactions that had taken place in connection with the GTRC need any explanation of the difficulties I had to encounter in attempting to initiate another state of things.

When George Reith made a mistake it was made on the grand scale. Both Reith men, however, worked to higher ideals and within greater competencies than their rages might suggest. Essentially they clashed with colleagues, especially those whose focus was limited to tidying up the minutiae round about them. These Reith men, however, looked ahead, and with almost visionary powers understood how the capabilities of the day might be transformed into the potential for the future. Inevitably they generated fear and discomfort among those of reduced vision around them, a state of affairs which they took pride in treating with a careless disdain.

George Reith would publish a report, to be distributed among the directors of the company in Canada, Liverpool and London. The Secretary to the London Board wrote to George that to do so would be inexpedient as it must surely lead to 'controversies and rejoinders which could not fail to prove detrimental to the interests of the Company'. To somebody of George Reith's temperament, this argument simply fuelled his resolve, so that the neatly printed document that he published worked as a more than adequate testimonial to his expertise as a financier, to his mastery of the trenchant sentence, but most importantly to his conviction that he, more than any, could lead the Company into future prosperity.

In his report, Reith asks whether 'the stream of commerce will find its way into the channel prepared for it to such an extent as is necessary to secure the success of the Grand Trunk and make it a paying concern? This suggests another question, viz: What is required to make it a paying concern?' A copy of this report in John Reith's enclosure volume about his father and grandfather follows immediately on from the Secretary to the London Board's caution about publication of this report. It's almost as though John Reith is joining in the laughter about the splendour attaching to the rebellious spirit, concurring with the attitude that insists on looking to the future with every move – and never mind the rest of them.

5

From Locomotives to Ships

George Reith was now realizing that his days with the Grand Trunk Railway of Canada – where he had so unreservedly cast his energies, asserted his views, argued his case and implemented, as far as was remotely possible, his chosen policies – were truly over; he had no choice but to accept the decision of the directors in Canada that he must resign. And so, in sad anger, he booked his passage back home and, with his trunk, repaired to the quayside in Montreal, to await delivery of the payment he knew he was owed. But since no payment arrived the liner must put to sea without him. There, on the quayside, in oppressively threatening composure, he continued to wait and to sit out further sailings, the telegram promised by Mr Blackwell for 11.00 a.m. that third morning failing to fetch up.

George knew of one thing in particular, about which there could be no argument. A balance sheet had been recently prepared for the shareholders which he, George Reith, could not approve and which he, therefore, refused to sign. He knew the figures to be exaggerated in the company's favour. This man Reith would never compromise his core beliefs and attitudes. And then, as he shifted his position on the quayside to make of his trunk something like a back rest, he went on to consider the occasion when he had been accused of initiating a reduction of wages in certain departments. The consequential hue and cry had been such that the directors cashiered, or dismissed him. But, he reflected, it's always, in such circumstances, a good idea to believe in the existence of a core of support somewhere within the organization. This had proved to be the case: he had discovered it most clearly and assertively located in the midst of the London Board of Directors, to whom he promptly appealed. While, diplomatically, they didn't actually say that he had been in the right all along, they treated him pecuniarily as though he had been. And when he prepared the report for which they asked, the result was diplomatically critical of the Canadian policy.

These were positive reflections of George's, out there on the draughty quayside. But still he must await the telegram from Mr Blackwell and the due pay packet. A ray of sunlight broke through the otherwise sullen skies, and put George in mind of a hopeful aspect to his apparently crumbling career. He had retained the Directorship of the Scottish North Eastern Railway; and while this would do little more than offer a part-time job, cordiality towards the company and the congeniality of its directors remained unimpaired. He reflected that it lay with those running a company to determine its success or failure. A sweetness attaching to these thoughts caused the craggy features to relax a little. Suddenly, he longed to be home, able once more to work actively towards a new start, and with relief walk away from the fruitless struggles of the past months.

With a certain guilt he thought of his own Jeanie, living out a lonely life in central Aberdeen. The position with the Grand Trunk Railway of Canada asked a lot of her for what had turned out to be no good reason. It was, however, only realistic to see himself, jobless and deeply frustrated, being a trial to his family, as he would be trying to fill his days in

41

the cramped accommodation of their little house in Chapel Street. Without a full-time job his many capacities would be stretched. He realized he hadn't seen his boys for a while at a key time in their professional development. Archie, now in 1859, was 22 and probably fully qualified as a medical practitioner. He would, he was sure, be struggling to extend his career to embrace his fervent Christian beliefs. Suddenly Archie's father felt himself to have been remiss in that he had abdicated his responsibilities. His own religious zeal caught up with him as he considered how his personal ambition had pushed aside other responsibilities towards his family. Indeed, he had certain guilty regrets that possibly he himself had had a calling into the Church, a vocation to which he had remained steadfastly deaf, in favour of the worldly aspirations which had found plenty of house-room with him. And then, after the boys Archie and George, came young Jean. However, concern for a future for the girl was in George's mind of a very different order from that which he experienced on behalf of the young men. Marriage and a family for Jean would be the reasonable expectation.

Eventually the Grand Trunk Railway of Canada was able to make a move which better reflected the resonance of its title. A messenger appeared on the quayside, spotted the gloomy huddle of the erstwhile Manager of Traffic, introduced himself, and handed over his package. George gave no hint of relief at his arrival and the end of his long and weary wait, but tersely required him to go and find out the next sailing for Port Glasgow, book him a first-class berth, and report back. Meanwhile George counted out the money he had received. On hearing from the messenger that the next sailing was not for two days, George then bade him find out the best hotel locally and book him in for two nights. 'To be charged up to the GTRC,' said George. Wearying of his usefulness, the messenger eventually returned, and somewhat sullenly handed over a note of the hotel and the booking. George had counted out the money delivered to him and, finding it to be all in order, gave the man a handsome tip and gruffly thanked him.

It was more than the prospect of his homecoming to which George looked forward with greater and greater urgency and which kept him buoyant in spirit throughout the discomforts of the journey. There was, he felt, in the hours of reflection to which he now unusually had access, an attraction – nay, stronger, a compulsion within him – awakening an excitement about matters maritime and connected to the ship-building industry. From his position forward on the ship and on deck he suddenly knew – as one can know as with an inspiration – where he would direct his energies and his search for information on his return. His excitement was inward, just as his contemporary Ralph Waldo Emerson was at that time writing in America: 'A man should learn to detect and watch that gleam of light which flashes across his mind from within.' He would make of the River Clyde his study and his focus. As to whether there might be job openings there he didn't know, other than that he would find one.

Back at home, George found himself trying to adjust to even greater challenges than he had expected. Jean, his wife, was anxious, excitable and much given to tears. The story that he was able, eventually, to piece together from her account about his older boy Archie was perplexing. He had qualified as a Doctor of Medicine and was a member of the Royal College of Surgeons. Further, he was physician to Aberdeen General Dispensary and had his own practice at No. 1 East Craibstone Street. But his religious urges propelled him into running the Sunday school at the Porthill School in Aberdeen's Gallowgate, a run-down area with very poor inhabitants.

Archie, moreover, had further self-imposed pressures: he insisted on experimenting with homeopathy, a discipline which was yet to gain status and medical recognition. (Later, Archie would be struck off from his position at the Royal Infirmary of Aberdeen). It was becoming clear to the father that his older son's balance of mind was unsure, given the pressures under which he worked.

For George, the younger of the two, a consistent picture of academic excellence was emerging. Aged only 17, he was intent on pursuing his apparent calling to the Church, with degrees from both Marischal College in Aberdeen and New College in Edinburgh. Here the father's reaction was far from straightforward: he had had to live with the guilt that arose from his own avoidance of a career in the Church.

And then there was Jean: she was younger than her brothers and her father's concern for her well-being and future was minimal: the girl, after all, would marry and have a family. Her future need give him no further concern. He would be much better employed working on his own future: he would need to familiarize himself with the River Clyde. He made up his mind to visit Glasgow and learn as much about it and its great river as he could.

6

George Reith meets his River

Very much aware that the post of General Manager of the
Clyde Navigation Trust was soon to be advertised, George
Reith was making a poor job at managing his impatience with
life in the restricted conditions at home. It was a modest house
which he and Jean shared in Chapel Street, Aberdeen. To
some extent he consoled himself, writing to as many people
of influence and distinction as he could, inviting them to
provide him with a recommendation for his job application.
He would back up his application with a booklet of testimonials from influential people. His booklet was printed for the
purpose and widely distributed among leading figures. They
wrote most fittingly of Reith as a candidate of distinction for
the post of General Manager of the Clyde Navigation Trust.
But now, in the cramped space of the Reiths' living room in
Chapel Street, the hand that held a diminutive envelope post-
marked Glasgow was shaky. George tore it open and eagerly
scanned the unlikely sheet that it contained.

Glasgow
8th March 1864

George Reith Esq.

Dear Sir,

I have much pleasure in intimating that at the meeting of the
Clyde Trustees today, you were by a large majority elected

General Manager, and I trust that the appointment may in every way be satisfactory and wishing you much pleasure in your new sphere of labour.

I am

Dear Sir

Yours very truly

M. McEwan,

Aberdeen

Scarcely a masterpiece of prose, this was a document which for George amounted to a certificate into a new life. Motionless, but with pounding heart, he stared out of the small window that gave on to backyards and heaped-up rubbish. George saw none of these; but instead that great river, its flow often hesitating to divide around islands of silt and debris, and then slowly resuming its twisting, curving route to merge with the sky as

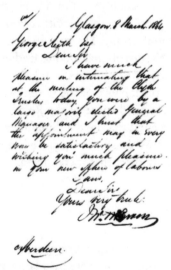

Reith's application acceptance letter, 5 March 1864

it found its way to the great open sea. Its journey would, he knew, embrace small fishing stations with their stone piers and slipways; and, well above the waterline, there would be leaning, tumbling cottages with mossed roofs and chimney pots slanted with age, use and weather. What was this scene that sprang so readily to mind? Why, yes. He had somewhere seen this captivating picture by one . . . Just now the artist's name had fled his mind. Nevertheless, he would go to Glasgow and he would search out not only the artist, but that place also. And many more. Ah! It was a picture of Govan Ferry; in his mind's eye, he recalled a fishing scene and in the distance there were farms and small industries; the river flowed on past the Fair Field and then round the island at White Inch and on past the country lanes of Scotstoun. Above rose the spire of Govan Old Parish Church on the south shore. Within George's inflamed imagination this scene of tranquil rusticity would, under his management, be transformed into many docks, quays, roads and embankments. And once they could so manage the river that it would no longer choke on the silt it carried with it, he saw great gantries rising up over ship-building yards. Quickly he would go and acquaint himself as thoroughly as he could with the places and people with whom the Clyde Navigation Trust must connect. He had always believed in the essential nature of preparation for any task. He would make of himself an apprentice for Glasgow and the work ahead.

Just then Jean came hurriedly into the room. Finding her man motionless before the window she at once jumped to the depressive position. 'George! What's happened then?'

'I got the job,' he said, briefly.

'Oh, the job?' Clearly Jean was not immediately connecting with that topic which had daily been behind George's every waking thought. Jean was not being stupid. Very simply it was that George had little or no inclination to share his preoccupations with anyone – not even his wife. Essentially a loner, the outside possibility that he might fail must be managed within himself. And so he had internalized his hopes and fears over many weeks, accommodating himself to their chastising nature and assuming an even more fearsome independence of outlook. Jean knew better than to enquire into this self-absorption and moodiness.

'William Simpson!' said George suddenly and out of no context other than that of his own abstruse thought processes.

'Who's he?' was Jean's understandable enquiry.

'Oh,' said George, 'he's a well-known Glasgow artist. I was recalling a fine picture he did of Govan Ferry on the River Clyde. You see,' he went on, at last coming to terms with his wife's perplexity and feeling that it was, after all, time he brought her in on things, 'I just heard that I got the job with the Clyde Navigation Trust.'

Jean, at last able to catch up with events, was warm and generous in her congratulations. George felt that he had been thoughtless in his estimate of her comprehension and that he should have discussed it with her a long time back. He was, after all, expecting her, without reserve, to move out and away from her base here in Aberdeen, with its proximity to her family, to tackle a greater city. And, to accommodate him, settle there and find some sort of life for herself.

It is perhaps not surprising that this belittling of women, especially the one with whom he shared his household and family, was an unfortunate attitude that he was again to hand down to a future generation. It emerged, unscathed, in the conduct of this grandson of his, this time within an era and culture in which it was less acceptable, even, than in that of Grandfather Reith. John Reith took on board these attitudes in bulk, it seemed.

Jean was eager for information and exchange. Her selected question – 'How did you do it, George?' – was perhaps not of the happiest, given that it was liable to more than one interpretation. But this time George wanted to do his best.

'Well,' said he, 'I saw this advertisement for General Manager of the Clyde Navigation Trust, and, to support my letter of application I wrote to as many people of influence and position that I could think of and asked them for a testimonial. I must say each was most generous. Then I had all their responses printed in this wee booklet, and sent it to the Chairman and Trustees of the Clyde Navigation, with copies for their selection committee. And – now – it seems to have worked!'

Jean took his collected testimonials from his outstretched hand eagerly, and between gasps and 'Oh George!' and so on spoke her admiration and pleasure. His booklet was entitled:

TESTIMONIALS
IN FAVOUR OF
Mr GEORGE REITH
APPLICANT FOR THE
SITUATION OF GENERAL MANAGER
OF THE
CLYDE NAVIGATION TRUST

Jean read from some of the glowing recommendations which rose up at her page after page.

The one that had afforded the greatest gratification to George was that from the London Board of Directors of the Grand Trunk Railway of Canada. These gentlemen described George as 'honourable, conscientious and painstaking; shrewd, sagacious in the conduct of business and tenacious of purpose'.

Charles Chalmers of Monkshill was an advocate and Chair of the Aberdeen Town and County Bank. 'I know no one whose inflexible probity, gentlemanly bearing, energy and practical business acquirements I could consider as better suited than you are for the post.'

George Thomson was a former MP and Lord Provost of Aberdeen. He wrote of Reith's 'untiring industry and very great ability in surmounting the many difficulties [of the railway] in the early years. His general intelligence and high moral character, which informed his conduct of business before Parliamentary Committees would serve him in great stead in the future.'

On they went, more and more in a certain concordat amounting to the highest endorsements of George's character and accomplishments. 'Here's my letter of application,' he said, putting that too before Jean. It would be interesting to know how far, in today's rapacious scrambling after qualifications, George's letter would have got him. But according to the standards of the day it was no doubt his ruthless honesty that won him the selection.

Among the accomplishments he listed qualifying him for the job to manage the Clyde Navigation Trust, he made these claims:

- experience in directing and superintending departmental arrangements and in guiding the movement of numerous employees;
- knowledge of accounting and of financial matters;
- many dealings with parliamentary business, and the arrangements necessary for carrying bills through committee;
- knowledge of the law (even though, as he admits, he is not bred to the law);
- experience in advising engineers and in suggesting ways in which works might be laid out and executed. (Again

accuracy must have its place: he would 'decline to take responsibility as an Engineer'.)

He is, he says, competent in writing up the minutes of the Board and its committees; and, finally, that if he is fortunate enough to obtain the appointment, it would be his ambition to conduct the business of the Trust *with the firmness and courtesy which contribute so much to secure confidence and command success'* (my italics).

One may speculate on which of the assets and qualifications that he listed won him the appointment. Given that he was not an engineer, which in itself could well have ruled out his application, what was it that so commended itself to the Selection Board? One might cite the dominance here of integrity; a conspicuous loyalty to the causes of the Trust, and to the well-being of its servants. Again, here is the question of leadership, without which follows unhappy bewilderment, loss of motivation and discontent. George had what it took to lead a workforce and engender devotion to the task.

A few days later, there he was, walking swiftly down Stockwell Street to Victoria Bridge, opened only ten years earlier in 1854, and spanning the river close to the fourteenth-century Glasgow Bridge. From time to time asking directions, George kept walking roughly westwards, and then was told to watch out for the spire of Govan Old Parish Church, and he would be there. At the Water Row, he was told, was the most hospitable Ferry Bote Inn, able to accommodate all a traveller's needs. No Glasgwegian would fail to notice the presence of a stranger in their midst, and respond hospitably.

Since the door of the church was partly open, and industrious sounds of sweeping and the shifting of heavy objects were escaping, George leaned against the door and entered, pausing to accustom his eyes to the general gloom. He picked out, in a pinprick of candlelight from one corner, a shadowy figure energetically at work in the midst of enormous stone forms, the like of which George had never before seen.

'Aye,' he said, by way of announcing his presence, and went on to apologize for startling this diligent worker. He moved forward into the encircling dimness – what was it about the ecclesiastical building which so readily put one in mind of gloomy hymns? – and held out his hand, saying his name also.

'Aye, I'm Tommy,' said the darkened figure, transferring his broom from one hand to the other and then using it as a prop. 'You see, I'm that lame. Got kicked in the thigh by my own horse so she did. But I'm lucky to get this wee job.'

And so they went on pleasantly conversing, George saying that he would be leaving Aberdeen soon to work in Glasgow. Pressed for his view on this subject, Tommy commented that was no mean job that he was taking on, and George didn't disagree. Meanwhile he'd come down here to get his bearings a bit, because Govan must be the best place to start.

Tommy took that as a signal to start in on his visitors' tour of the district. 'Did you know,' said he, 'that hundreds of years ago the Clyde was such a small river that she was never more than fifteen inches deep? She was no more than so many tiny burns that tried to make their way around islands and banks of silt. In those days you could make your way from Govan to Partickhill dry shod. Mark you,' says he, with a wry grin, 'many's the folks that fetched up on the other side drenched all over, their language blue. Not everyone was good at hopping from one island to another. Then somebody had the idea of a flat-bottomed boat that could make its way from south to north shores. Better still when they attached a chain to it and dragged it to and fro. Then – at last – somebody says: "We must dig out this river so that it can flow properly." As far as

I can tell they're still at it the now; and if they're not digging it's because they're just arguing, the city fathers, that is, about how to do it. But still it's only the little shallow boats that can make it to the Broomielaw.'

George had heard Tommy with close attention: this same theme was presenting itself again with greater-than-ever emphasis.

The pair had moved out of the church and were making their way down the Water Row, the slipway that led into the river's murky drift out to sea. 'Your rivers in Aberdeen will not smell like the Clyde does, I'm sure,' said Tommy. George agreed that the smell was bad, not at all what he had expected; 'There'll be no sewage system,' he supposed, to which Tommy agreed, 'even though more and more folks are coming to live in Glasgow; and again more arguments getting nowhere to solve the problem'. George meanwhile was further building this new information into his developing strategy for the Clyde, amused at the circumstances in which it was taking shape.

But Tommy was going on energetically to point out other sights of significance. 'This is the Doomster Hill. Folk say that that was the meeting place of the Moot, nearly 900 years ago.' He explained it was a location for the outdoor assembly of people where political and legal matters were discussed with the dempster, or legal officer, in charge.

Tommy rattled on, leaving George free to engage with his latest preoccupation: all the greatest ideas that he had had for the river – its commercial development with quays, wharves and docks, its ship-building yards and its huge industrial potential – depended on navigability. This shallow, sluggish, smelly, meandering collection of wee streams amounted to little service as they were. The potential of the river, with its marvellous access to the western seaboard, had somehow to be realized. This great initiative was to be one of George's achievements. Everything depended on dredging. Then George was visited by fearsome doubt. Suppose his thoughts on these things were mistaken? He had, after all, no experience of rivers and their ways, of the manner in which dredging might be introduced and sustained. A strong man and a determined one, he was in the unfamiliar territory of self-doubt. He had everything to learn about his new job. Thousands would be depending on him.

But Tommy must get back to his cleaning: there was to be a wedding in the church that afternoon. But, said he, had Mr Reith not seen the sarcophagus, nor the hump-backed stones in the graveyard? Mr Reith was starting to wonder when he might be free to resume his own quest for information, for which he had travelled all this way. But good manners and an appreciation of the generous attention that the church officer was bestowing upon him left no doubt that he would again accompany him up the hill into the graveyard and back inside the church building.

'Here we are,' Tommy said, as they re-entered the gate. 'There's thirty-one of these early Christian carved stones here. Ninth century, they say. And there are four tall prayer crosses to give you stories from the Bible for folk who can't read; and, now, here's one of these "hog-back" stones: they're marking graves, like.' Now, quite caught by Tommy's enthusiasm for his charges, George bent over the nearest 'hog-back', felt the coarse texture of its narrow humpbacked form, and noticed the stone beasts that clambered up at either end. He remarked to Tommy on the sides of each with a design resembling roof tiles. 'Now,' said Tommy, 'you must come in to see the greatest of them all.'

In a corner of the church his candle was still guttering faintly; with its help he lit another, then proudly held it up beside a very large lump of sandstone. George found himself doing some fast learning in an unfamiliar territory. Bending down near the flickering light of the candle, he started, with the help of his fingers, to feel out some of the patterns of interlaced strands that raced along its sides. Then, with growing excitement, he found that he could discern many vigorous creatures on the move, such as two horses busily grooming one another on one of the panels.

Tommy was enjoying the response of his apt pupil. 'Can you guess what it is?'

George rose stiffly from the stone floor, as undeniably cold as it was damp. He shook his head in some bewilderment. 'No,' said he briefly. 'Tell me.'

'Well' – Tommy was delighted to oblige – 'they claim that it's a sarcophagus, a great stone coffin. For St Constantine, they say.'

'Oh. Who was he?' George was about to wonder how far he would be able to keep his tail up in the face of his own invincible ignorance.

The ever-willing Tommy obliged. 'He was St Constantine; he probably died here in the sixth century. He had been a king in Cornwall – I'm told that they have plenty of places down there named after him – but his young wife died. He took himself off to a monastery in Ireland where he stayed for seven years. Then they discovered that he was a king, and all they could think of doing was making a priest of him. So he crossed the sea to Kintyre to meet St Columba. But there he was killed by assassins. Afterwards they named several places after him. There was Kirkonstantine which became Colmonell. And this kirk here is called after him. And now, what do you think, but that they're going to pull it down and put up another in its place!' The eloquent church officer's rage was plain, and to demonstrate his point he dug his broom handle into the wall beside him. 'See!' said he. 'Sound as a bell.' He rubbed away at the black mark left by his broom handle on the wall, but to little effect.

'It's a lovely spire,' said George, 'pointing the way here.'

'Of course,' resumed the other. 'Quite so. And what do they do, but go off and find a so-called architect who's not even from Glasgow, and knows nothing about us folks, but likes to build posh like, for the ones who are very grand. Why couldn't they look to our own architect men? The likes of . . .' – and here he found himself in deep water, having inadvertently committed himself to a list of those prominent in the field in Glasgow – '. . . the likes of David Hamilton and the chap Rochead,' pronouncing his name with some difficulty. Here names dissolved into gestures. 'They build for us, they do. And then we've Mr Honeyman and Mr Thomson,' said he, relieved to find some more names. 'Fine modest churches they would put up for the folk of Glasgow! But no. You'll see what kind of a monster building your Edinburgh fellow will come away with.'

Clearly, Tommy's rage was fuelling itself, pleased though he was to be able to release some of it in this manner on to his sympathetic listener. George decided not to ask the name of the offending architect who had got the job in Govan; it would be well known soon enough.

Time he reconnected with his visitor, thought Tommy. Astutely he remarked that Mr Reith would be away to meet Mr Charles Randolph and his partner Mr John Elder at the Randolph and Elder Engine Works. They were, he thought, in Centre Street in Kingston.

George acknowledged the accuracy of his prediction and, with directions supplied, set off again, as it were, upstream to the famous Engine Works. But not without most cordial thanks to Tommy for his time and his information. He had, he said, as they gravely shook hands, given him plenty to think about.

'Well,' came the rejoinder, 'when you're up there in your new office for the Navigation Trust, see and give those magistrates and town councillors, and, too, those fat tobacco lords plenty to think about as you tell them what you're going to do to rescue this sick river, with all its shoals and its stench.'

He waved his broom handle so aggressively as to make clear how much he would like the job of instructing the Board of the Clyde Navigation Trust himself.

Amused and stimulated in equal measure, George set off, knowing that he would make sure that, come what may, he would carry out the injunction with which he had been sent away by the church officer of Govan Old.

7

George's Self-imposed Apprenticeship Course

George Reith, by inclination and experience, operated prag-
matically. Now, however, he found himself invaded by an
unfamiliar dimension to life: that rather uncomfortable
realization of history itself, of a long, socially shared past,
tapering away back into the mists of time. A past that was so
ancient that little of it was susceptible to verification. He had
stumbled on this appreciation through his chance encounter
with Tommy – he of the broom handle – who was himself so
seized by his patch, its antiquities, and his responsibilities, as
to be able to engender an excitement in even so preoccupied
a listener.

Later that morning, as George strode along towards
Tradeston in the Kingston area of Glasgow, he understood
how slow he had been to engage with what Tommy had
wanted to share; and that, when at last he had been able to
break through some of that resistance, George had appreciated that this, his first visit to Glasgow with his work – or
mission – in prospect, would remain shaped by this unex-
pected introduction. He had come with a view to anticipating
the future, and instead had met up with the past – the deep
past, with all its emanations. Now these two dimensions must
feed and inform one another. At a very basic level George

58

knew that ancient Govan would always be imprinted on his mind as a result of the experience of his significant first visit to Glasgow – even if, rather oddly, it had amounted to the introductory session of his self-imposed apprenticeship. If, he thought wryly, someone were to enquire as to the content of that apprenticeship, they could be forgiven their surprise should he try to explain that the initial session had amounted to a brief study of St Constantine.

Charles Randolph was one of the founders of shipbuilding and engineering on the Clyde. The firm specialized in the construction of steamship engines, through which the Pacific was one day to become within reach of the Clyde. As George approached Centre Street in Tradeston, he saw the unusual building that marked the renowned partnership of Charles Randolph and John Elder. The building was vast, and perhaps, even from without, expressive of its purpose. 'The Randolph and Elder Engine Works' was the bold sign that asserted the presence of this small empire of invention. He found a side door in the midst of huge ashlar blocks; this door was on a scale to accept human, as opposed to mechanical, traffic. He pushed it open, and was at once halted by the scale of the construction before him – aside, even, from the intense industry emanating from so many work stations around its perimeter. The interior was constructed on cathedral-like proportions: iron stanchions and brick piers supported colossal timber beams. It was, indeed, an arresting experience just to stand there and observe. One or two men started to notice his presence, and he knew that he must explain himself.

'Mr Randolph,' he said, 'he's here, is he not?'

At once arms waved him in the general direction of a tall man, well-whiskered, who was clearly consulting in turn with each of his staff, touring the premises to do so. Spotting George he crossed the floor space between them and, with hand held out and welcoming smile, believed that the visitor must be Mr Reith. It was as though Reith had been expected. If Mr Reith was surprised he managed to cover it up. He knew, of course, that Charles Randolph was a Trustee of the Clyde Navigation Trust, a position the said Trustee proceeded to confirm with the assurance that he had been a warm supporter of Mr Reith's candidature as General Manager. Now, so soon after his appointment, how honoured he was by this visit. He motioned to George to join him on a nearby bench, and waved to one of his men to request he bring them a mug of tea each, and to help himself as well. At once George picked up on the courtesy with which this distinguished engineer treated his men, the assured route, he firmly believed, to loyalty, a dedicated workforce and the steady progress of the firm and its discoveries.

'So!' said the genial host, turning to George in anticipation of an energetic exchange. 'What do you see as priorities for the river and its burgeoning industries?'

'I should wish, at this stage . . .' said George, struggling not to sound pompous as he picked up on the older man's patrician style. He started again. 'I would greatly regret it should I fail to gain the benefit of your opinions at the very outset. I intend to work here for the good of the Trust, as your servant.'

There was a thoughtful pause from Charles. 'All right', came his cheery response, at length. 'It's the river, isn't it? It's got to be our jolly old river. It's dredging, and more dredging, and more. It's putting in place a system whereby the force of the river is made to act on itself to keep it scoured and able to maintain a consistent working depth so that vessels drawing seven feet can move upstream to the Broomielaw without fear of shoals and sandbanks which unpredictably shift their position and catch the mariner unawares. Mind you, there's nothing new or very original in my view. Chaps have been fidgeting with this one for nigh on six hundred years. But the difference, the importance is *now, the immediate future*. There is a new urgency. Things are quite, quite different now. I do believe that, for the first time ever, what with your advent and all, we can look forward to the launching of ships of a size and magnificence that no one has yet dreamed of.'

'Aye,' responded George, keen to hide the emotion he was experiencing. 'But those launches would have to be a wee drop further downstream than here.' He made his remark without a trace of amusement or eager anticipation. Within, however, his heartbeat quickened and he longed to start in on the job that very day. 'Aye,' came again, as a sort of space-filler. 'What couldn't we do with a river with steady flow and consistent depth?'

Charles responded with warmth. 'What indeed? We are struggling in our workshop towards the development of a steam engine so that the Pacific Ocean will be within our reach without the need for refuelling. First, however, we've still to make it possible to leave the Clyde without the most ignominious groundings on any one of these—.' He swallowed rather than spoke the colourful epithet that attached itself in his mind to the said shoals and sandbanks. No doubt, a man both sensitive and tough, he had already picked up on a certain stern asceticism in his chosen candidate to run the Trust.

'Of "the Free", no doubt,' he said to himself. His was of a more liberal disposition: his grandfather had been a surgeon, 'out' at the '45' and imprisoned in Carlisle Castle for his pains. His father was a printer and bookseller in Stirling and author of a history of the town. There, at the high school, Charles received his first education, passing on to the high school of Glasgow, and thence to its university.

'There,' continued Charles, never entirely able to suppress his humour, although aware that, with so intense and serious a listener, you would be as well to label any remark as 'joke' should it have a humorous tendency, 'I took classes in Latin, Greek and Logic. But they never stood in my way.' He twinkled across at his listener's impassive face.

'What's your preference, then?' asked George, much taken by this arrestingly alternative approach to life, so very different from his own austere background, reinforced in him by the exacting teachings of self-denial of his chosen church.

'Well,' said the other, 'I was always passably good at science. It seemed to fit. And the results you see all around you here. But,' he continued, a little nonplussed, 'you didn't come here to talk about me. I very much want to know your views on so many of these things. Ah! Here is my partner, John Elder. He's spotted the tea on the go,' he added mischievously. 'John, this is Mr Reith, soon to be General Manager of the Navigation Trust.'

George and John Elder shook hands gravely, and George explained what he and Randolph had been discussing; that is, the prime task in relation to the river and its industrial priorities. He added that he was encouraged to learn that the main concern was the varying depths of the river and of persistent reefs and shoals, resulting in its failures as a navigable waterway.

'Our work is in vain unless we introduce dynamic change,' added Charles in summary. Charles summed up that, with the hope of dynamic changes, we foolishly labour away. He waved his arm, warmly proprietorial of his whole workforce.

Quietly insistent, George returned to his point. 'While warmly endorsing these views I would like to share my further perplexity with you. Staying, as I did last night, and will again tonight, at the Ferry Bote Inn, my expectation of a good night was much modified by the discovery that the river runs by as an open sewer. It stinks as it pollutes and as it spreads disease. But now that I am concerned with such a question, and any others that might follow, I certainly trespass on your time and programme. Perhaps, gentlemen,' said George, with deferential politeness, 'you might be good enough to join me – and, indeed, with one or two others of the Trustees of your choice – at an evening meal tonight at the Ferry Bote? But,' he added, suddenly gripped with doubt as to the extent to which his lack of training in good manners was about to let him down, 'I overstep the mark. I am in no position to take initiatives, even of the simplest kind.'

Charles, whose liking for this rugged character from the rural north-east was steadily growing, warmed further to him for his uncertainties as well as for what were already lining up to become his convictions and his aims. He said he would be delighted, and would send messages to two of his fellow Trustees. John Elder, meanwhile, excused himself on the grounds that matters internal to the Trust would be under consideration, and he was not a Trustee. Before George left, however, Charles Randolph would take him on a short tour of his premises and productions, explaining, as George well knew, that their objective was the development of a steam engine that worked out of compound cylinders, of differing sizes, with the steam led first into the smaller of the two, and then into the larger, before being condensed and returned to the boiler. In this way steam consumption – and therefore coal consumption – was reduced by half, and global destinations could be reached without refuelling.

'My colleague John,' said Charles magnanimously, 'is the brains behind this. The final product will be his triumph. I am one of those privileged to have passed through the Napier – Elder school. David Elder,' he said, shooting a quick glance at his companion, to assess the extent of his familiarity so far with this roll-call of great names, 'was one of the most accomplished mechanics that ever held a place of trust in any workshop on the Clyde. And as for Robert Napier, as well as his achievements, he is the kind of man that it does us all good to know. It's exactly ten years ago that we engined the *Brandon*, our first ever equipped with the compound engine.'

George had a hearty dinner that evening with his invited companions. With pipes lit, the Trustees proceeded, for the benefit of the newcomer, to unravel the saga of the river and its problems. The Trust had been in existence only six years – since 1858 – and had 25 Board members. The current Lord Provost of Glasgow was chair, with nine more members being magistrates or councillors of the city. Another nine were directly elected by the ship owners and ratepayers, with two more chosen by each of the Chamber of Commerce, the Merchants' House and the Trades' House. Of the Trustees accompanying Charles Randolph that evening, one represented the ship owners, and the other was from the Merchants' House. Between the three of them they produced an oral history of the range of the initiatives and experiments undertaken down the ages to clear the river of its shoals and its sandbanks.

It began with the need to locate a harbour for Glasgow in the city centre. In the 1640s they started way down at Port Glasgow; the problems and costs associated with the so-called road between Port Glasgow and the city centre were considerable. That was the time when the tobacco trade with the American colonies was developing well. Certainly, there was competition from London; but many times, while the Thames ships were still beating about in the English Channel, a Glasgow-owned ship had reached Virginia and was loading. Here, as you could imagine, the city fathers were all buoyed up by their success, and even in 1662 developed harbour facilities at the heart of the city at the Broomielaw.

Listening to this, George was looking with mounting appreciation from one to the other of his well-primed informants. His colleague, James, wanted a shot at the narrative: 'So! In 1806 they set about building the quay at the Broomielaw; they did it with such zest that Glasgow's historian, M'Ure, as I remember right, described it as being "so large that a regiment of horses may exercise thereon".' This quotation was delivered by James with a certain obvious satisfaction. George, however, reached across to the log basket in the grate and carefully placed two logs on the embers. The crackling attracted the attention of the barmaid, who was now reminded of her added responsibility that night, and bustled in.

'Oh, don't worry,' said George, 'the fire is doing fine; but thanks all the same.'

'Maybe you's all would be ready for a drink?' She smiled beguilingly at them. When it was George's turn he responded that he was fine, although, on second thoughts, a mug of tea would be welcome. The others ordered up their whisky, Charles keeping his thoughts to himself, hoping attitudes of the 'Free' wouldn't curb the style of this otherwise good candidate for the post with the Clyde. Charles was still ready to appreciate Reith, especially as, to his inner amusement, he noticed George's obvious endeavours to imitate the style and manners of his immediate company. 'Of course,' thought Charles 'they're only the efforts that we have all had to make to feel socially included.'

The talk resumed. George was perplexed. He wanted to know what kind of a craft would be able to navigate the Clyde – never mind the new harbour – in the state it was in, in order to beat the others across the Atlantic. Sometimes they were all speaking at once as they picked up on the developing story. Especially as no one could find the precise answer to George's question, they would instead answer questions he hadn't asked.

It was that road to Port Glasgow that was making it imperative to attend to the river's interests once more. And it was their own interests that they had principally in mind at the time. As a result, the city councillors were finding themselves heavily leaned upon to open up the river to regular traffic, and so they appointed one James Stirling as consultant for the task. He was a mathematician with an inventive mind – not to mention a deviousness which had led to a colourful past. He was so bright that he got himself an appointment at Oxford University. But his Jacobite sympathies were in his way. Off to Venice he went, where his inquisitive mind again caused him trouble: he discovered the secrets of Italian glass making, for which a second expulsion, this time by the Venetians, followed. He was pleased enough, therefore, to accept the offer by the Scots Mining Company to manage their Leadhill Mines in the remote village of that name in the Lowther Hills. Here, with his inventions of water wheels, sluices, drainage systems and so on, he was usefully employed and won himself a more stable reputation. Sufficient, that is, for his services to be sought by the Glasgow magistrates, who discovered him working close to the source of the Clyde. The field of endeavour in which they looked was, after all, sparsely populated; at that time the band of civil engineers was small and select and, as to river management – such skills scarcely existed.

Nothing loath, therefore, James Stirling applied himself to the problems of the city magistrates in his accustomed style, able to convince them at the outset that he would need to conduct a survey of the stretches in question. His survey amounted to walking up and down the banks for a bit and making mental notes. On this slender basis he moved towards his recommendations: that weirs and dams should be built across the width of the river, thus increasing its depth upstream, and making it accessible for coastal vessels at least.

Plausible enough, it must nevertheless have been apparent to the meanest mind that the question of navigability to reach the said enhanced upper stretches of river was as yet unaddressed. But James Stirling was able to walk away with a presentation silver tea kettle and lamp engraved with the Glasgow coat of arms. Trading with the Colonies opened up with the 1707 Act of Union. No wonder the excitement at the Scottish trader loading his tobacco before ever the English were properly put to sea. The group nodded approvingly.

'And so, what happened next?' came the quick follow-on.

'Bad times.' Glasgow had been taken for a ride by that fellow Stirling. Years later it took a visit by John Rennie, to condemn all these planned weirs and dams. And Glasgow was so poor it couldn't feed its own.

Now Gordon of the Merchants' House took up the story. What happened next was that, in September 1768, they found John Golborne. His skills and experience were genuine. Things improved. His aim was to reduce the width of the river so that it ran faster, and as a result with a new capacity: that is, itself to carry much of its own silt out to sea. This he did by building dykes at right angles to the banks, so that the force of the river, now enhanced, might act on the river bed. Thus the river itself was carrying quantities of material out to sea. Not content with his success so far, Golborne invented a kind of primitive scoop, or dredger. It was the most ramshackle arrangement you ever saw. But Golborne was not going to be found wanting in any area of experimentation; and so this odd contraption, like a sort of spoon, was worked by three men in a barge-like vessel, with all manner of ropes, stays, pullies and so on. While not particularly effective, its chief virtue was the encouragement of having a man working for the City who was keen to innovate and try out new ideas.

Despite the lateness of the hour George was keen to open up the discourse to the area of dredging, not to mention its associated themes: sewage management and disposal. An account in the *Glasgow Weekly Magazine* in the early 1770s reported that 'three coastal vessels arrived lately at the Broomielaw directly from Ireland, with oatmeal, without stopping at Greenock to unload their cargoes'. Such an event caused sufficient excitement that, along with several of the magistrates, merchants and townspeople turned out to watch. Vessels of 70 tons or more gingerly made their way upriver for the first time, and into the city. Mr Golborne was rewarded, and not only with another piece of engraved silverware: remembering that this expert engineer was always on the move and unlikely to have much use for a silver kettle in his luggage, the City added a cheque for £1,500 as well.

There were still layers to this story to be unpacked before ever they might reach the themes of George's urgent enquiry. Thomas Telford too played a part. Telford was a little critical of Golborne's work, because it was clear that between the dykes the sediment was building up fast. He suggested that more could be made of the tidal flow, and that this might be achieved by joining up the ends of the dykes as they projected from the shore with longitudinal or parallel training walls. The tidal force would thus be increased, to the advantage of the scouring action.

Talk then went on to James Watt. He was instrument maker to Glasgow University and, when taking his famous walk on Glasgow Green, had been hit by the idea that was to result in practical steam power. In 1802 the *Charlotte Dundas* was built on Watt principles. She successfully towed two barges on the new Forth and Clyde Canal – that is, until she did so much damage to the canal banks that the owners objected and the practice had to be discontinued.

Then came the irrepressible Henry Bell. His wife was owner of a hotel in Helensburgh on the Clyde coast. He introduced a novel way of transporting new hotel clientele along the Clyde from Glasgow out to Helensburgh. The steam-powered *Comet* ran out from the Broomielaw in Glasgow to Renfrew by way of Helensburgh. However, paddling her way downriver, she stuck fast on the Dumbuck Shoal off Renfrew. There was nothing for it but that the obliging passengers must climb out, push her off, and quickly climb aboard again. To Bell's credit, he was very enterprising, but *Comet* was an oddity of a craft – round and squat and propelled by paddles. Henry Bell and his ship would be remembered for some time to come.

'Now, George,' said Charles, 'the night is wearing on and we must leave you. But first, if I may enquire: you may possibly have plans for your next moves? I have wondered if we can introduce you to our new Superintendent of the River. He has succeeded James Spreull in that position and, although that's a hard act to follow, I, for one, am hopeful that we may have found our man in John Clark. Would you like to meet him?'

George responded eagerly, remembering at the same time the influence of Mr Spreull. His reputation had extended well beyond Glasgow for his many years' service to 'his' river. He had died suddenly, George had heard.

Charles explained that, apparently, somebody had dreamed up the idea of a dredger to speed up the scouring of the river bed, but Spreull was so devoted to Golborne's dykes and training walls scheme that, no sooner had he heard of those 'smoking mechanical monsters' – the dedgers – than he died, allegedly of the shock. There was nothing he wouldn't do for his river – except, it seemed, that.

On this sober note, the evening – a most memorable one for George – closed, except for an arrangement through the ever-helpful Charles Randolph that George should meet John Clark the next morning on the north bank of the river, at the slipway for the Govan ferry. Tired, but satisfied that a start was under way, George retired to his room and to his evening's devotions, persuaded that the hand of the Almighty had been at work with him in the day's doings.

8

George Meets Some of the Early Shipbuilders

When George boarded the Govan ferry the next morning at the Water Row, it was already almost full to capacity. Designed for vehicular traffic, it had one horse and cart already aboard, an accommodation to which the patient animal in question was clearly already accustomed. This was in contrast to the next, this time a nervous youngster who sensed danger ahead and refused to drag his load up the ramp. This kind of scene was by no means unfamiliar to George, and he watched how the driver treated his beast, reassuring and encouraging; and, when at last safely aboard, offering the reward of a carrot. 'A good tip here,' George was thinking. 'Beasts are not so very different from people.' Never off the job, he was considering the virtues of leadership. It would certainly mean treating everyone well, as far as possible; appreciating every effort and, where possible, incorporating ideas offered as important initiatives to be followed up. George's personal preparation for his forthcoming tasks and challenges was now a daily feature of his life; he would, after all, be starting his job in a few weeks' time. At this moment, however, his attention had switched onto matters of a practical nature: it was not immediately obvious, as the ferry cast off from its southern mooring at the Water Row in Govan, in what manner she was propelled.

Moving about the ferry, George tried not to draw too much attention to himself as he conducted his unobtrusive enquiry. It was obvious that the exertions of two of the crew who were strenuously at work on a winding engine on deck were essential. Through a rotating cog a chain passed to work a form of traction. This chain was fixed, well secured on either bank, and able to resist the current. This much was clear to George as he peered over the side, weighing up the advantages of this mode: it was able to accommodate vehicles, in contrast to those of the rowing-boat ferries, at Whiteinch, or others working upstream out of Glasgow Harbour, at York Street and at Clyde Street. He noted in passing the surprising endurance of ferries operating so close to the ancient Glasgow Bridge.

Here they were now at Pointhouse, where a small crowd was gathering for the return ferry journey. George scanned the figures for that of John Clark, the River Superintendent he had come to meet. Now – this must be he, detaching himself from the group and then, a little deferentially, waving in what was intended to be George's direction. Ashore, the two met and exchanged greetings. John Clark suggested they repair to the Pointhouse Inn in order to plan their day to George's advantage.

John had prepared a very rough sketch map, as he apologetically explained, to give an idea of the layout of the significant ship-building and dock-yard developments to date on that north shore. Mr Reith, he felt sure, would wish to acquaint himself with a slip dock. One was to be found upstream at John Barclay's yard; it had proved its usefulness these 40 or so years, making possible an endless stream of repair work brought about by the damage done to ships' bottoms by the many sandbanks and shoals which persisted in the river. And, if Mr Reith would like, he might visit the newer Tod and MacGregor yard across the Kelvin further downstream at Meadowside.

'It was a great event,' continued John, losing a little of his customary reserve as he continued to enjoy the rapt attention of his listener, 'when Tod and MacGregor's amazing dry dock was opened six years ago, in 1858.'

George knew he must ask this amiable man about the importance of a dry dock, how it functioned and how it was managed. This he did on their 20-minute walk upstream to Stobcross, to the Barclay yard, a comparatively short distance from the Broomielaw itself. Mr Barclay had favoured this site because a deep pool off-shore might allow him to build and launch large boats. 'A man packed with drive and ambition,' remarked John, more to himself than to his companion; but a useful pointer nevertheless to the meeting ahead.

Reith, however, already had an observation to make: this yard was almost certainly too close to the Broomielaw – Glasgow's harbour-to-be, as he saw it – for the benefit of either enterprise. Since Barclay's go-getting ways had become the local talk, John Clark was keen that they seek him out, in order for Mr Reith to establish some kind of an understanding with him, putting his questions to him directly. Instead, Reith enquired of John Clark about his own immediate task as Superintendent of the River, and the preparation for it.

'It was of the very best,' said John, glad to be asked. 'I was for many years deputy to James Spreull, a man for whom the cause of the river and its navigability was his life. A hard act to follow,' said he modestly, 'although at the same time the very best preparation.'

George shot him a quizzical look, behind which was the question: after so luminous a start with James Spreull, what sort of a job was this rather self-effacing man capable of achieving?

They were now arriving at the Barclay yard. Introductions were completed, and George planted a few well-articulated questions firmly into the exchange, quietly insistent that the undivided attention of the forceful shipyard manager was required here. Looking him firmly in the eye, and making it clear that he was no man to be trifled with, George announced his need fully to understand the purpose behind this innovation of the slip dock.

Back came the answer: Mr Reith would be aware of the navigational hazards of the river at present, with shoals and sandbanks that could seldom be avoided. The result was that many ships with damaged hulls put into the yard, with repairs best carried out by hauling them up on cradles onto slipways for dry, detailed inspection below the water line. 'This,' added John Barclay the proud father, 'was my son Robert's idea; we are never short of work with these facilities at our disposal. The only alternative had been for damaged vessels to return to Port Glasgow for underwater repair. As you will appreciate, our provision is preferable.'

To George it was obvious that John Barclay was making no reference to his rivals downstream.

'Our main business, however,' Barclay continued easily, 'is shipbuilding.' He explained the benefits of this site for the purpose, at which George, aware of the credit that is to be acquired by terminating an interview with an abstracted manager sooner than expected, decided that time was now up.

For a moment, John Barclay was disconcerted that he was being given no further opportunity to explain his aims, innovations and successes; and that this masterful character, having got what he came for, was now already pressing on to his next engagement. But he, Barclay, would need to be wary if he was not to find himself at a disadvantage. What was that which he had caught from Mr Reith about his prime objective, at the moment, being the deepening of the river and the removal of its shoals and sandbanks? John Barclay felt a mounting anger as he began to see the danger to his lucrative slip dock repair business.

George, for his part, had been well aware that his off-hand remarks about dredging the river would have a combustible effect on this man whom he considered arrogant and combative. Far from regretting his response, he had been, he knew, willing to assert his position and views with a customer who would be only too willing to dispute authority in any form. George meant to continue as he had begun.

John Clark repeated his suggestion that a visit to Tod and MacGregor's yard here, at Meadowside, could be an advantage. 'Although,' said he, 'John Barclay made no mention of it, he must be aware that this firm are pressing ahead in the dry dock business, in a more progressive manner than the Barclay scheme, even though they only opened six years ago.'

'I think I pick up from you,' said George, 'that despite their newness on the scene, they probably have the advantage over our friend Barclay? However, I do assure you, John, that I see my task here as offering a lead in favour of progress, for the benefit of all – as soon, that is, as I find myself in such a position as might justify such an outlook – and by no means one in which unwittingly I foster antagonisms. Now, what distinguishes Tod and MacGregor, would you say?'

By now the two had reached Kelvinhaugh, bordering on Yorkhill, and John was explaining, a little apologetically, that they would soon need to board the row-boat ferry to cross the River Kelvin. His companion, however, as always eager for new experience, quickly made light of this.

'To start with,' said John Clark, 'David Tod and John MacGregor have had the inestimable benefit of a certain rivalry with David Napier, and I've heard it said of him that he is the greatest pioneer of stream navigation. This, for the first time being anyway, probably puts them in the lead in that field, as well as enabling them to berth between sixty and seventy vessels a year in their dry dock. Now,' he said, interrupting himself, 'Washington Street is behind us, and number twenty-eight was where Robert Napier, cousin of David, first opened the Vulcan Works, a number of years ago.'

But George was interrupting him. 'Yes, indeed. Robert Napier assumes the leading role in Clyde shipbuilding. No doubt we will be calling him its "father". These Napier cousins move like shadows ahead of us: I long for the opportunity to meet them both. We will be building up the status and reputation of the Trust on the achievements and status of Robert and David Napier. What an opportunity for any man, to be thus positioned between two world leaders in any field.' This last he spoke as though to himself, his imagination and excitement again gathering momentum. Now he was mumbling to himself: 'From sail to steam; from wood to iron; what a time to be here on the Clyde. But' – and here his tone changed a little – with all these accomplished engineers I fear the river is producing more than it can accommodate.

'I don't know what you think,' said George more loudly, becoming uncharacteristically voluble in his elation about the Napiers. 'I don't know what you think about the efficiency of this rather cumbersome so-called slip dock system that John Barclay was so pleased about. Labour intensive, I thought.' He explained his view that it would be by no means impossible to work on a scheme that could become a dock that was really 'dry'; an off-stream dock from which the water might well be extracted by three or four steam-driven pumping engines, leaving the ship secured by horizontal as well as perpendicular beams and safely accessible at all points above and below the water line. It was hard to believe that nobody had yet thought of a solution that was both manageable and effective!

John Clark, who, after all had not been in post all that long, was starting to wonder how well he might be able to measure up to so testing a situation with this man Reith, who clearly expected everyone to be operating at the top of their form all the time, a condition in which anything less would be seen as regrettable inadequacy. Clark however, was, like so many more to come, stimulated and excited by the advances made by the Napiers. David Napier, whose reputation rested on his skills as a marine engineer, as well as on his well-developed business sense, had been responding to the increasing need for foundries and workshops for the building of steam engines, for boilers and gearing and shafting elements. With steam navigation the need for such workshops increased. This would become the early stages of the route leading to heavy engineering, in which the Clyde was to lead the world. David Napier's career had started in an obscure corner of east end Glasgow, on the Camlachie Burn, where he had carried out those improbable experiments in nautical design from which he went on to build his first marine engine.

It gave Clark great pleasure to retell David Napier's story. He opened engineering works at Lancefield on the north bank in the 1820s; and in them he had installed a fitting-out dock, which was a small tidal basin where ships might lie afloat, clear of the main river traffic, as their engines were installed. But then a terrible thing happened to him. Experiment, and its consequent risks, was always at the heart of his work. He had installed his new 'Steeple' engine in the *Earl Grey*, then in Greenock harbour; there was a terrible mishap, and she blew up, with loss of life. David felt he could no longer hold up his head in Scotland, and he went south to London. He would be an old man now, John concluded.

George, for all his toughness and irascibility, was much affected by how a brilliant man's story had ended calamitously here on Clydeside. He was silent as they walked several yards. 'That's terrible,' was all he could manage to say without revealing his emotion. John Clark remarked to himself on the oddity of a man of apparently ruthless drive who was yet, emotionally, so vulnerable.

Gathering himself together, George changed the subject. 'But back to your remarks about the opportunities around the building of a *real* dry dock, such as you described. This is to be found here at Meadowcroft, by the same firm, Tod and MacGregor? We will introduce ourselves and go to inspect it.'

The two now entered the yard; a few men watched them as, under Clark's guidance, they made their way towards the water's edge. On the way, however, they were drawn up short by a loud and friendly hail.

'Hello, John Clark. Why, it's you! What brings you here?'

John quickly introduced George: 'This is David Tod,' said he, 'and this,' he continued, 'is Mr George Reith, soon to be General Manager of the Navigation Trust.'

'Ah, Mr Reith!' said David Tod, instantly genial. 'You are surely most welcome. We've all heard that you are joining us here on our smelly, dirty old ditch of a river.' In his jovial tone, he continued, 'And how pleased I am that you've come to meet us here!' But, he wondered, would Mr Reith be interested to see their great new dry dock?

Mr Reith was indeed interested. So much so that, a little further on, as they turned a corner around a great gantry, George gasped. And then, typically and disconcertingly, he remained silent.

Allowing for a decent pause, David made his understatement. 'We can take nearly the largest merchant vessels in existence,' said he, 'but we can't quite take the Thames built

Great Eastern yet. As you can see we have no shortage of customers.'

As George looked down into this constructed abyss, the dry dock of Messrs Tod and MacGregor, he remained as still as the gantry next to which he stood, in a visible silence.

This, understandably, was disconcerting to David Tod, and also to John Clark. Not yet fully conversant with the ways of the world in leadership and executive power, they both felt ill at ease with this grim-looking person who was lining up to assume power over that river. This great new dock was their pride and joy and a huge business risk. To the young David Tod, it now all seemed questionable in the face of the reaction that their great construction – nay, invention – was apparently provoking in the mind of this grimly enigmatic figure unexpectedly arrived on their scene. What this young man could not have known, as he wrestled with sudden self-doubt, was that Reith was not at all dismayed by what he saw. In fact, relatively speaking, this silence was a positive reaction. And now, the amazement that overtook Tod was of a very different nature.

This tall, crusty figure was ponderously turning round towards him; although he did not smile, his hand was held out with a certain compelling insistence. 'Well done!' emerged from out of the whiskers and prominent chin. 'My warmest congratulations to you and your colleague. You have achieved something on which I myself had set my heart. You must allow me now, if you would, some of the questions that are already fermenting within me.'

David could do little more than take the offered held out hand with its warm powerful grasp, and mutter his wish to respond to any question as well as he might.

'That ship, lying off-shore there: is she booked in for repair here in your graving dock?' asked George, using the alternative, descriptive name for the dry dock. He continued, 'She is of no mean tonnage or indeed length. You must be clear that you can accommodate her.'

'Ah yes,' said David, with swelling pride. 'She is the 1,150-ton *City of Glasgow*, one of our very own. She inaugurated the regular service between the Clyde and New York in 1850. This service has recently been augmented by the even larger *Edinburgh*; we can accommodate both of these ships in our graving dock here. The problems that arise are not to be found here,' he went on with justifiable pride, 'but downstream.' He explained that, after a perfect launch (about which both he and Macgregor had been very nervous, given that it was the first one ever), their *City of Glasgow* was held up by grounding. She had to sit it out over at least two tides, something which was very much not in their interests, and certainly not their responsibility, but which affected their reputation for speed and reliability.

He continued, a little nervously now, 'I've heard it said that the trade of Glasgow is well ahead of the capability of the Navigation Trust to cope with it.' No sooner were the words out of his mouth than, in youthful fashion, he clapped his hand across his face, appalled at what he heard himself say.

'I see,' said Reith. 'So you are telling me just what are the priorities of this Trust which I shall shortly have the honour to try to direct.'

David's embarrassed denials acknowledged acceptance of his social gaffe.

'No, no,' said George, entirely unruffled. 'I am here to learn from those who, like yourself, are at the forefront of this whole Clyde enterprise. My authority, and that of my fellow Trustees, would be indelibly weakened were we to follow up on our own preferences and ideas, making them our priorities, rather than those which are born of trials and experience of people like yourself and Mr MacGregor,' he ended rather stiffly. In no way given to introspection, George, in replying to David's unplanned outburst, was responding to the young man's eloquence, a style which George himself regularly used. It was seldom anything but useful to disconcert people, even as he, George, himself had so nearly been just now.

'I take it,' asked George, 'that your water source for this great dock is the high tide?'

'Yes,' said David. 'Although preferably the spring tides, when the process of refilling the dock with its close to five million gallons can best be done. After that, the ship is comfortably secured on both bilge shores and on side shores – these are the wooden distance pieces that keep her thoroughly and safely supported for men to work on her below. When the dock is emptied, these are the conditions under which the tasks can be most rapidly completed. To empty the dock we have four steam-driven pumps working centrifugally; the dock is emptied in two hours. The power house is within that compact tower beside the lock.' Tod pointed. 'Down here is where the keel is housed within a cradle. They are a refinement which we were encouraged to adopt, in order to be able securely to accept all manner of size and design of ship. We have no doubt about their value. The travelling crane, over there, is itself of inestimable value, especially for situations connected to the final fitting out of the ship. Or in the unlikely situation in which it becomes necessary to remove a boiler. We all have much to learn, still,' he finished, 'in the ship-building, maintenance and repair scenes.'

George was now pronouncing himself well satisfied with all the new information, and appreciative of David's time and care. Handshaking completed, and about to start out of the yard, George had another off-the-cuff thought to put to him. 'Tell me,' said he, 'if this is not an unfair question: what would you and your business partner feel if the Navigation Trust were to plan itself to construct, say, a six million gallon tank, to take, even, the likes of the *Great Eastern*? My guess is that such a dock would be five hundred feet by sixty feet across, with a depth of twenty feet. Would that affect your trade, even though you are already averaging so very many ships – sixty or so a year, is it? Obviously I would want to talk this through very thoroughly; and if, in the future, my Trustees favoured the idea, we should next seek a meeting with you and your colleague. Our business in the Trust would be to support, not undermine, such magnificent initiatives as I have here experienced today.'

David responded, 'Just now I must thank you for the courtesy of raising the matter with us in advance.' He was struggling for his answer. 'I would be less than honest if I did not confess that there are times when John and I worry about the possibility of power failure in this very new and untried enterprise; and that in such a case it must be that your idea of a public facility would be for the good of the river and all its many users.'

Thus concluded this significant meeting, apart from more handshaking and good wishes all round. No sooner were they out of earshot than John Clark watched carefully for the unguarded reaction he was needing to test the reaction of the Navigation Trust's next General Manager. He got his answer in Mr Reith's demeanour, which, while not exactly jocular, exuded a certain robust satisfaction.

John asked him if he would like to see more.

'Why, certainly,' replied George, with unusual warmth. 'This is all of the greatest use to me before I start work. I am indeed most obliged to you, Mr Clark, for your expert guidance to the sites where significant enterprises are at work. So – where next?'

Despite the oddity of Reith's form of address, John was deriving a sturdy satisfaction from his labours as guide. 'Well,' he said, 'you may be surprised to learn that our next meeting, provided he is on the spot, will again be with Charles Randolph!'

'That does not surprise me,' responded George. 'I saw him, certainly, as a man of great drive and ambition, but I hadn't thought it possible for him and his partner to work two yards. I had seen Randolph and Elder, certainly, as specialists in the construction of steamship engines; but now – are they embarking on shipbuilding as well down here?'

'Yes, that is, on the south bank, for which we will need to board the Govan ferry again.' John continued, 'That's exactly what they are up to. Last year they found that their Govan site was inadequate but they found the Fairfield Farm, half a mile downstream, for which I gather they paid handsomely. Mr Randolph, I understand, is thinking of retiring soon . . .' but George's attention was taken up by a familiar voice welcoming him to the giant engine workshop.

'My dear Reith,' it said. 'How do I find you today? Making a quick dash to look around here before I retire, eh?'

George responded, as ever, with hefty dignity: 'Mr Randolph, I may be new to the Clyde, and with everything to learn; but of one thing I became convinced as I came along here with my excellent guide: that I must visit, even briefly, what is surely about to become the largest and the greatest yard on the Clyde, while yet the influence of its presiding genius is in the midst. "Clydebuilt",' he went on, 'that is what they will say of your ships, and it will be spoken, with honour.'

George was investing great gravity into the exchange. But if that was his style, and that of Charles was always lighter, there continued to grow between them a mutual respect and understanding. 'Come and see inside,' said Charles. 'While we are here, you would be interested to call in on the yard in which Robert Napier worked until 1841; and then finally the Thomson Brothers' new yard.'

Even as he conducted George around his Fairfield yard's impressive premises, Charles wanted George to learn more about Robert Napier's sojourn, a little further upstream at Govan West. During the time that he was there, the most amazing partnership with Samuel Cunard had developed. Cunard had the idea of founding a steam packet company, whereby a regular mail service would be opened up between the Clyde and America. Sam had been a wily old bird, who had spotted Robert from across the Atlantic, and very quickly the service was in place, with Robert's ships crossing and re-crossing the Atlantic. 'You know, George,' said Charles, 'it's high time you were meeting up with Robert Napier. None of us lives for ever, and he has been retired for some years now. You will find him living with his most hospitable wife at Shandon, further downstream. Believe you me, he will be expecting your visit.'

George's desire to meet Robert Napier burned ever more firmly within him. But, for now, he and John simply looked about them as they walked on to their last meeting of the day, with James and George Thomson. George remembered that theirs had previously been a yard on the north bank of the river at Stobcross, one of several which he had noted as certainly being too near the Broomielaw and its future development as Glasgow Harbour. These two ambitious brothers had moved across to the south bank, to Mavisbank, where they were just now packing up for the day. The brothers were clearly interested to meet George, he at once picking up on the characteristic drive that they shared. As well as this showing clearly in their demeanour on meeting this significant stranger, their talk tended to be of both liners and battleships of unprecedented size – for which, they considered, they might have to remove again back to the north bank and to a site of ample scope at Kilbowie, north of Clydebank.

No one that evening, as they bade one another farewell, could have understood the scale on which this firm, even though under new management, was in future years to work. The Thomson brothers were to be bought out by their chief creditor, John Brown of Sheffield; the result was the largest liners the world had ever seen, and the little hamlet of Dalmuir translated into Clydebank, as the need for the increasing workforce to be housed locally developed. Perhaps it was a blessing for George that this shining future for his river could not yet be apparent to him. It would, after all, be beyond his lifetime.

George Reith

9

Meeting the Ancient City

'By the way – have you got yourself somewhere to live yet? You can't just go on putting up at the Ferry Bote Inn!'

George was somewhat nettled by Charles Randolph's shouted message as he and John Clark were leaving what was to become the Fairfield Shipbuilding and Engineering Company. He shouted in reply that his priority was the Clyde Navigation Trust. Once these most useful preliminaries had been attended to, with John's help, he would then be able to consider his own domestic arrangements.

Tomorrow, thought George, he would find his way to the house recommended by Randolph in Queen's Crescent and view the outside and the area in general. And then he would also devote the day to familiarizing himself better with Glasgow itself.

The next day, having established that Queen's Crescent was on the north bank of the river, he crossed by the Glasgow Bridge and soon found himself in the midst of the commotion of a fast-developing railway network. This was the city of Glasglow Union Railway viaduct. Drawn as ever by railway activity, George positioned himself as near to the building activity as he safely could. He watched the bustling, clanging hurly-burly with rapt attention. In particular, he was fascinated by the expertise of those engaged in the laying of railway lines, such as those that had just completed their crossing of the river by the new, specially constructed, bridge adjacent to the early Glasgow Bridge.

George Reith, with his height, fair hair and distinctive features, was never going to be anything other than a conspicuous figure – something he often regretted. He was getting himself noticed now by a certain passer-by, who also seemed to want to observe all the din and exertions as closely as he. Noticing that he and this tall spectator apparently shared an interest, the stranger held out his hand to introduce himself to George, remarking that it seemed that they were both captivated by all this bustling agitation before them. The stranger was John Tweed, and he was presently engaged in compiling a guide to Glasgow and the Clyde.

Tweed explained that all the work going on before them represented a major enterprise. This was a station connected to a rail terminus. The great gathering of girders, stanchions and angle irons would one day also be used for a large concourse in a prestigious station. The huge foundations to the right already suggested no mean building – a very grand hotel. But Tweed was wanting to impress the visitor. He pointed out the foundations for a gracious and very grand staircase leading out of an imposing entrance hall. The architect, likely to be Rowand Anderson, had previously designed the new building for Govan Old Church.

George explained that he was about to be the Clyde Navigation Trust's General Manager.

Mr Tweed kept his thoughts on this to himself but volunteered, 'There is, however, something greatly to be regretted about this railway site.' He recounted its early history, his eye still on the scene before them. This had been the old village of Grahamston – a mix of single-storey cottages and dwellings. How rapidly and apparently easily the railways were invading and usurping the living stories of the city's past! While he talked, he made a mental note to include the story of Grahamston in *Tweed's Guide to Glasgow*.

George, meanwhile, was recognizing that his new role would similarly challenge a treasured past. Modern progress, led by people like Charles Randolph and his prospering engineering company, as well as David Napier's premises in the vicinity, would change the face of the city. This idea of a past and all the material signs of its nature was so new a revelation to George that he could not but experience his own aspirations in rail and in shipping in conflict. And here, in what had been the village of Grahamston, he wondered passingly what happened to its inhabitants.

As if to rub in the point, John Tweed reached into a pile of rubble that was before them, and with both hands lifted out a boulder which had clearly been crafted as a small window lintel. 'Here you are, Mr Reith,' said he, with a sudden access of familiarity. 'Think of all the folks who for many years would have opened and shut their window here for the weather.'

Keen to change the subject, George asked Tweed if he could very kindly give him directions to Queen's Crescent. Mr Tweed, intrigued to have encountered the man likely, before long, to become a leading figure in the life of the city proposed that he be permitted to lead George by a circuitous route to St George's Cross. His intention was to introduce him to one or two of the city's greatest surviving testimonials to its medieval past. George, ever eager to learn as much as he could from as many people as he could before he took up his new position, was only too happy to accept.

The two set off in an easterly direction along the Trongate, which at Glasgow Cross becomes the Gallowgate, the longest street out of Glasgow with a destination all too clearly signalled by its name. At Glasgow Cross there stood a high steeple

attached to a seventeenth-century townhouse. With enthusiasm he pointed out the steeple's wonderful Gothic crown that
holds 'musical bells', like many others in Scotland.

George was much in awe of this exquisite monument to a
bygone age, and as he looked around at the context in which
it must now survive, his eye fell on another sign of a vibrant
past. He pointed out a small Gothic tower and learned that
it had belonged to an even earlier church, that of St Mary
and St Ann – the first Reformed church of the lower town.
The church had been destroyed by fire in 1793 and all that
remained of the earlier church which had been rebuilt in a
simple modern style was the tower.

Tweed explained that the renowned Dr Thomas Chalmers
carried out a most distinguished ministry at the church. Dr
Chalmers had laboured in the face of invincible ignorance
and immorality and was famed for his magnificent oratory.
The squalid and poverty-stricken conditions in which people
tried to live might, to some extent, explain their lifestyle.
Chalmers raised generous sums of money towards the allevia-
tion of such great poverty. In later life, Dr Chalmers returned
to the University of St Andrews to take up the Chair of Moral
Philosophy.

This narrative reminded George of the noble movement
which Chalmers led, which culminated in the Disruption of
1843. He was impressed to be acquainted with the spot on
which this great man had laboured to free the nation from the
tyranny of a system of patronage in the appointment of ministers to parishes – a system, George thought to himself which
rode roughshod over the wishes of the local people.

Mr Tweed now pointed out the famous Saracen's Head
Hotel. Dorothy Wordsworth stayed there with William, her
famous brother, when they toured Glasgow in 1803. She had
been much taken by what was becoming known as Glasgow's

New Town, then spreading out westwards – the fine pale stone of which it was built, and the businesslike bustle of its people. This reminded Mr Tweed that his favourite author, Daniel Defoe, had noted when writing his *Journey to Glasgow through Scotland* that it was 'the cleanest, beautifullest city I have seen in Britain. It stands deliciously on the banks of the River Clyde . . . The four principal streets are the fairest for breadth and the finest that I have seen in one city together. The houses are all of stone . . . ' Here Mr Tweed's verbal memory began to fail him, but he carried on nonetheless about the Doric columns with which most were adorned, 'adding to the strength as well as the beauty of the building,' he concluded triumphantly.

Wondering whether, at this point, he had driven his exegesis too hard, inadvertently silencing his guest, Tweed pointed vaguely eastwards, along the Gallowgate. 'That,' he said, 'is one of the longest streets in Glasgow, in this direction passing Camlachie and proceeding to the open fields where are to be found the city's gallows.'

At the mention of 'Camlachie' George responded enthusiastically, remembering that he had once been there, as a child, with his father. It was the location of George's encounter with Napier many years ago. The man's experiments with ship models of varying designs was still vivid to George. At first sight he had been puzzled to find a grown man playing, as George had thought, with toy boats. But this clever man was studying the models' varied behaviour in the current; he was searching for the ideal design for ships' bows. At the time some unkind journalist, more ignorant that he knew, wrote up these experiments as 'resulting in the wrong end foremost'. 'Little he knew,' concluded George ponderously, 'how great were to be the implications for the future following this man apparently sailing toy boats for his pleasure on the Camlachie Burn.'

George was, even now, starting to grasp the thinking behind the design of the great liners of the future. The greatest of them all was to be the *Queen Mary*. Into her audacious design would be incorporated a pioneering inward sweep of the massive bows. As a result, with each majestic downward slide her bow would ride deep into the troughs of the waves, and would be followed by the long, unhurried, upward climb over the next travelling roller, the spume furies endlessly chiding the magnificence of her Napier–Camlachie designed prow.

They moved on up the High Street, passing the university to reach the cathedral. 'Housed within the boundaries of the university colleges,' Tweed said, 'was the Academy for the Fine Arts. Robert and Andrew Foulis were the founders. They were printers to the university and keen to train artists and craftsmen and to improve taste. You will see,' he said, as they approached the crossing of the High Street with Duke Street, 'how pleasant are the green areas round about: the orchards, the vegetable plots and the common areas where the animals graze. The university itself, even, has two quadrangles, presided over by a tower, for which, Sir, I know you will share my admiration. All this verdant territory encouraged our first historian, McUre, to write of the 'pleasant, odoriferous smell of flowers and fruit which filled the open and large streets'.

There would, however, have been plenty of other smells. The housing was dense, arranged in arcades, or 'piazzas' as they were called, with tall tenements or 'lands' rising high above them. Behind them also stood wooden-fronted buildings. These, unlike the buildings housing the clergy higher up the street, had no gardens. The street was indeed too thickly populated, and standards of hygiene hadn't been considered, as the populace left its dung and rubbish to accumulate until carted away as manure. Such were the conditions that confronted Dr Thomas Chalmers as he laboured away in their midst. George was curious to see into such spaces as might exist between the wooden-fronted buildings, and was amazed at the ways in which the houses jostled one with another. Here the children played, while the mothers gossiped together or sat out on their steps, especially when briefly the sun might break through the rooftops and the overhang above and bestow a little temporary warmth.

Returned to the High Street and the fresher air of the green spaces, George merely remarked on the terrible conditions some folk must endure and bring up their children. He wondered how the finer folk teaching at the university felt about bringing their families here to live among it. Mr Tweed responded that George had most accurately described one of the principal woes of the university; such, indeed, that moving to another site was under discussion. George's gaze fixed on that gently authoritative stone tower, as though it stood in watchful attendance on the two university quadrangles and the green of the orchards beyond, which together justified Glasgow's title, 'The Dear Green Place'.

Tweed said that there was now a threat of removal of the university buildings. They had been in the High Street for two hundred years! The Foulis brothers opened their college in 1753. Now the university was in financial straits and would find it hard to refuse the Glasgow and South Western Railway's offer to buy their land for use as a marshalling and goods yard.

George was silent. The High Street continued to wind its way up what Tweed described as the glen of the Molendinar, rounded a bend and became Castle Street. Then St Mungo's Cathedral rose up before them both, in all the discreet splendour of the medieval idiom.

George, still trying to accustom himself to modernity's onward march, this time in the form of the railway, stopped and stared. Somehow, he must again face up to this conflict of ideals. He was beginning to feel most acutely the value of antiquity and the ringing past. Into these reflections now moved the ancient cathedral itself, in quiet ceremony, grown up and out of the green valley of the Molendinar. The struggle in George's mind was now becoming an attempt at a resolution of the part to be played by industrial progress in the survival of the city. These, however, were thoughts which he did not yet care to share with his guide, who was now, despite the failing light, urging his companion to come with him for a glimpse of the cathedral within.

Entering by the west door, they found the soaring nave illuminated by the soft glow of candlelight. Together, in reverent hush, the two walked up to the fifteenth-century stone screen, their footsteps echoing high in the vaults above them. At the crossing steps rose up to the choir, while others on both sides led down to the elaborate vaults of the lower church, the original building, said to be connected to St Ninian and the cemetery that he consecrated. Here also, tradition held, was the grave of Fergus, who had had a part in the founding of the cathedral on this spot, and around whom arose legends of the miraculous powers of St Mungo.

Then the two returned by the west door to the outer world and the clatter of horse-drawn traffic. George thanked John Tweed cordially and, following his final directions for the last leg to Queen's Crescent, set off in the insistent twilight. Now his domestic concerns began to intrude on his thoughts, not least his sons, Archie and George. But above all, he realised as he strode along, he could not settle in Glasgow without being fully conversant with the legends around the holy man Fergus and the part played by St Mungo. More significant even than the impact of modernity upon antiquity was the confrontation he was experiencing of the ancient faiths with contemporary drive and invention.

10

The Belle of the Glen

'The Belle of the Glen', they called her. She was Jean Stuart, born in Glenlivet in 1809, the daughter of a small farmer, James Stuart. Unusually for the Glen, he was a Protestant in a community of Roman Catholics, descended, he maintained, from the Royal House of Stuart. But Jean, an exceptionally pretty little person, on whom George Reith's eye was eventually to fall, never found any evidence to support the claim to so distinguished a lineage. George, for his part, maintained a lofty disdain for the rumour – even though his wife-to-be seemed rather to enjoy it.

One Sunday at the kirk, Jean had noticed this conspicuous young man in the midst of the congregation and was impressed by his height, his fair hair, and his serious look. For such earnest church-goers there was no doubt that it would be at church that they would meet again; and in due course, in 1834, they married. During the time that George worked in his brother David's office, he and Jean lived modestly in Aberdeen, in a small single-storey house off Chapel Street, a narrow way that led northwards off the western end of Union Street, before turning off to become Kidd Street. Matilda was their maid and loyal friend through the harrowing experiences of births and cot deaths, infants, toddlers and sickly youngsters.

Between their sons David and John Stuart, who died aged one year and four years respectively, came Archie who, along with his younger brother George, survived. More losses were to upset Jean's slender equilibrium. Alexander, born in 1846, died the following year; James Stuart died aged four; and then Joanna died in her first year of life. That this woeful story was in no sense unusual at the time does little to dilute our sense of the devastation that must have been felt by so many families with so little protection against child infections.

Named after her mother, Jean was their last child. She survived and became the source of some of the impressions we have of life in the household of George Reith, with his ruthless ambition, and his wife, most gentle, lovable, but of an uneasy balance of mind. What is clear, however, is that George adored his wife, and that, however great the demands on him of his professional life, it was together that they faced the trials of family life.

Jean, the youngest, wrote to her cousin John Reith (actually her nephew but addressed as 'cousin' as a fond familial term), who worked to model himself on his grandfather's severe style and achievements. Young Jean noted that, as her mother's features in old age were clear-cut and beautiful, she must have been a beautiful girl.

It was not long after the death of George and Jean's baby, Joanna, that George set sail for Canada, on his erroneous mission to run, as he supposed, the Grand Trunk Railway of Canada. It may well have been at this time that his wife had a nervous breakdown, a state that was loyally attributed by her surviving daughter to an overdose of mercury. Things improved for the family when, out of a large field of applicants, George became General Manager of the Clyde Navigation Trust. In 1864 he and Jean moved into the house at 16 Queen's Crescent in Glasgow, which George had inspected. In those days, it was one of a neat crescent below the Cowcaddens, then on the western extremity of the city. There they were able to live more comfortably and spaciously than before, with, following the custom of the day, a modest troop of servants.

Now Jean was able to recover much of her charm and her love of life. She made friends readily and they came to visit her, to enjoy her affectionate nature and hospitable table. A decanter of port always stood on the sideboard. Drink was something George regarded as a necessary adjunct to his new station in life but it was something that he would take only when duty insisted. He had experienced his parents' deterioration from its effects. Furthermore, two of George's brothers had lost their lives as a result of their excesses. Thus it was noticed that the level of port in the bottle on George's sideboard went down very slowly, in this otherwise welcoming household.

George was not always as attentive as he might have been but he was steady in his affection and admiration for his wife; her encouragement to him was unstinting. She would often accompany him to the many public functions and dinners which, in his position with the Navigation Trust, he must attend. 'They made a most handsome couple,' their daughter remarked. When, later, one of her grandchildren was married, and this particular grandson, John, led his grandmother up the aisle, she remarked that it seemed to her as though 'Grandpapa's mantle has fallen on you!'

There was 'the spooky side' to Grannie which included the second sight. She said she had always known when death was coming to the Glen, and described a little hunchbacked old lady dressed in brown, seen sitting by the side of the road, rocking herself to and fro. And then there was the tale of the shepherd who, after dark, was hastening off the hill, back home to where his wife was expecting a baby. But at the last bridge before his cottage he was startled to see his wife standing there, dressed in white and holding her baby, wrapped in a long white shawl. When he reached her, arms outstretched, she vanished. In his cottage he found his wife, dead, holding her dead baby in her arms.

One morning at Queen's Crescent, as Jean came downstairs, she said that she knew that 'something was wrong with Maggie', a relative to whom she was much attached. She wondered what it was, and was much distressed. At that moment, the doorbell rang. A maid answered, and there stood a telegraph boy, his bicycle propped against the outside railings. He had a telegram, which the maid received and handed to her mistress. The message was that Maggie was dangerously ill. Maggie died soon after.

There is also the tale of Grannie Jean being bothered by the sound of horses and carriages passing her window. She looked out but saw nothing. The next afternoon, the same events took place, with nothing to be seen. But on the third afternoon, when she looked out, there was a funeral passing, all those black horses with black plumes, drawing a black hearse. These experiences afford anything but peace to those who experience them, especially as they are so often completed by all the discomforts of realization.

Was Jean, so clearly a home maker, also a good mother? Very probably, in that to have been careless of these nurturing relationships would have been quite contrary to her nature. But as to how it was that women, given the trials and the risks of birth, could then go on to survive the almost certain loss of at least one of their young, and face up to further pregnancies, with their accompanying hazards and discomforts, is past imagining. Of eight births, Jean and George brought up three survivors: Archie, George and Jean. Despite her already nervous disposition and her husband's absence abroad, Jean learned to endure.

Without doubt she would have been invigorated by her sons' successes, both at school and in further education, and later in their careers, Archie in medicine and young George in the Church. But the latter was once the cause of no small embarrassment to his mother. When visiting the Glen and being entertained by her relatives, the small boy objected to eating his porridge with a wooden spoon. 'My mother has silver spoons,' he announced to the toe-curling embarrassment of his parent. He later objected to drying his face on a towel, 'the kind my mother dries her dishes with'.

With some domestic damage to be repaired, George was able to supply his disconcerted parents with evidence from the Aberdeen Grammar School, which he attended between the ages of 11 and 15, that he was no ordinary pupil. William Eyre Grant, Rector, reported in shining terms, going on to say that he entertained 'a confident expectation and lively hope that the proper manner of his mature years will be fully acquainted with the promise of his youth'. One might think that after such an eloquent testimonial there was only one way to go, which was backwards – some evidence of which was borne out by a letter from the young man to his mother reminding her of his own forthcoming birthday! This letter was written when he and his sister Jean accompanied their father on a surprise return visit to Canada, which took place between his reconnaissance visit to the Clyde and the taking up of his appointment with the Trust.

George's academic career took him to Kings College, Aberdeen, Marischal College, Aberdeen, and then New College, Edinburgh. In his New College studies he learned of the pre-eminent scholarship of the German kind, and planned a session at a German university. His father, as ever intervening inappropriately in his son's career, feared the 'loose-minded doctrine' that his son would encounter, and even more the 'easy-going customs of the German city'.

Finally, young George made it to Erlangen in Bavaria, where, for five months he could delight in the fully stretched exercise of his intellectual capacities. In addition, George made a lifelong friendship with Robert Lorimer, a scholar of no mean distinction.

This friendship brought to an end a disturbing time of confusion and depression for George. 'My parents had dedicated me to the Ministry at the Disruption, and I was never allowed to forget it. When I had finished with the University and several tempting offers were made to me, I hesitated for a little, much to my father's alarm.' Young George must further be treated to a veiled rebuke for his absence abroad: 'Your mother', wrote his uncomprehending father, 'is sad in the evenings, as she misses you so.'

At New College the young man, very much more socially inclined than his remote father, enjoyed the company of his fellow students but found himself being 'seriously admonished' as he said, by his father 'for your late-night habits and partying' and for enjoying the company of those with 'seriously liberal opinions'. The father did not ease matters for his sons. His letter is dated 1864, when he was on his early visit to Glasgow to familiarize himself with aspects of his new appointment; he wrote from the North British Hotel in Glasgow. He went on, with heavy piety: 'that is a false liberality that is more liberal than God's own truth'. After more of the same, he affirmed that 'Mama will again be left lonely'; young George, meanwhile, again finding himself in an unenviable position.

George's older brother, Archie, at the same time was intent on putting himself through a similarly rigorous training, in medicine. In later days, Aberdeen was to erect a memorial to him for his tireless work among the poor and deprived of the city. His youth was spent during the stormy years of the religious ferment which swept through Scotland in the early 1840s. This was the moment within the Church when it was freed up from the system of Patronage connected to the appointment of ministers to parishes. The new system was being espoused with mounting fervour: such appointments would no longer remain the prerogative of the land owners and the heritors to choose and impose their candidate upon the local population, since this deprived the local community of any democratic opportunity.

The older George Reith clearly remembered that his great-grandfather, Alexander Reith of Clachanshield, well endowed with the Reiths' natural capacity for eccentricity, in the 1730s had been attracted by the newly minted doctrine of the Revd Ebenezer Erskine. He preached a vehement message from the Church of the Holyrood in Stirling, that 'no congregation should be beholden to the gentry for their sole right in the choice and appointment of the local minister'. Added to which, it was well known that the Reith forebears existed in a state of contumacious tension with their local heritor, 'the Barclay of Ury', as they scathingly called him. Thus, the struggle arose between those of the evangelical persuasion in the anti-Patronage movement, which led to the Disruption of 1843. George, father of Archie and George, imposed upon them both a religion of the stern ascetic type, in which was embedded the passionate desire to 'fulfil all righteousness'.

Archie's family had worshipped in Holburn Parish Church, Aberdeen, under the Revd William Mitchell, who left the Establishment at the Disruption in 1843 and led his Kirk Session and congregation to their regular worship in the open air on the nearby Justice Mill Brae. In due course, as a young man, Archie graduated as a Doctor of Medicine and member of the Royal College of Surgeons. He was appointed one of the physicians to the General Dispensary, later becoming a junior physician in the Royal Infirmary. But it was his devotion to the controversial new science of homeopathy which, after four years with the Infirmary, brought about his dismissal from that appointment. The upset to the young doctor was in no way confined to his family circle, but sent large reverberations throughout the medical world of the day.

Archie was, moreover, under another compelling influence. His work with the General Dispensary had brought him up against the harsh reality of the unrelieved wretchedness of areas such as Aberdeen's Gallowgate, and the squalor, vice and crime that characterized life there. Archie's attention was drawn to the old and crumbling Porthill School and the possibility that, through the generosity of a local philanthropist, it might be demolished and rebuilt. Archie involved himself in Sunday school work there, pursuing his aims with such zest that the school developed weekday programmes as well as its Sunday school, with him as its Superintendent. Seriously overworked, he turned down his father's invitation to join him, George and his sister Jean on their visit to Canada. Archie's commitments, chiefly to the Porthill School, made his absence impossible.

Recovery from the ignominy of having lost his post at the Infirmary eventually followed, to some extent, for Archie. His friends and associates rejoiced at his marriage to Margaret Skelton. For a number of years he carried on, as far as time would allow, a private practice from 1 East Craibstone Street, with his responsibilities at the Porthill School extending to teaching the children reading and writing during the week.

He founded, with others, the Aberdeen Medical Missionary Society. He battled with a typhus outbreak until the loss of his wife Margaret, very possibly through an infection carried in by Archie. This, once more, brought him up against depression. He was left with grief, five children and overwork. After over 30 years' dedication he reluctantly, and in great distress, gave up the school, perhaps on his mother's advice. Amazingly, however, he married again. Oddly, soon after his second marriage – we don't know his new wife's name – he took a cruise alone to South Africa; but arriving in Cape Town with no sign of solace, if that was what he was seeking, he set sail at once for home. On the *Norham Castle* he was far from well and when, at last, the cliffs of Dover came into sight, he lay down on his bunk. When the ship docked in Port Glasgow a few days later, they found him dead in his bunk.

But it was by no means a life lived in vain; homeopathy has never again been denigrated as it was in Archie's experience. His selfless work among the heavily disadvantaged in Aberdeen's Gallowgate opened up new channels for social improvement. No wonder the city erected its memorial to him adjacent to the site of his greatest endeavours.

Meanwhile, George, his younger brother, with his seriously successful academic achievements, chose to start his work among those of Glasgow's citizens for whom life was a wretched affair. Behind the frontages of Glasgow's High Street lay the city's Wynds. No doubt influenced by Dr Thomas Chalmers, who, in the midst of his congregation in the ancient Tron church, had poured inspiration into the cause of the Free Kirk and its expression in the Disruption of 1843, the Revd George Reith accepted an invitation to work among Glasgow's deprived.

Leading industrialists of the day included a deeply committed Lord Provost, one Robert Stewart, who succeeded in his dream of replacing the noxious drinking water taken straight from the Clyde, with fresh water conducted into the heart of the city from Loch Katrine, through 13 miles of tunnelling and 25 aqueducts. Charles Tennant made his fortune with the St Rollox Works which produced a bleaching agent for textiles, soap and glass. The works' situation, only a quarter of a mile from the cathedral, while providing employment for many, also polluted the atmosphere to such an extent that, at last, a chimney was built in an attempt to distribute the particles more widely and thus reduce toxins. 'Tennant's Stalk' was at least 435 feet high. John and James White were members of the Free Church who were also committed Liberals and philanthropists. But they remained indifferent to the conditions under which their employees must live and work as they ignored social improvement in their endeavours. The Revd George Reith associated himself closely with many of the evangelicals' initiatives.

It was into this scene of industrial process, called 'progress' – except by those who must suffer from its effects – that George Reith senior, in due course, led a formidable contribution from the banks of the River Clyde. At the same time his son George struggled to try to alleviate the miseries of its workers.

Jean Reith, nee Stewart, of Glenlivet, wife of George Reith

11

George Reith Assumes his Managerial Role

Being such a robust character, it seems unlikely that George Reith cared about his public image as a bossy man. To him, performance and leadership were very important. Whatever, else, George Reith was a man in authority. What mattered was the completion of the task to the highest standards possible. His aim would be to push back the boundaries of invention and innovation. So much so that the particular characteristic of his – bossiness – was observed by an increasing public with amused enjoyment. The word came to define the man and his role: a local magazine called *Fairplay* (17 December 1886) described George Reith as 'the bossiest man on Clydeside'. George, however, did not enter into the amusement.

His remit, as he began his task as General Manager of the Clyde Navigation Trust, was, however, enough to have daunted anyone. The Trust had taken over from the earlier River Improvement Trust. As well as having a greatly enlarged field of responsibility, it was now expected to tackle the many and vociferous complaints about its failure to represent many of the trading interests of the City. There struggled a lively suspicion that, within the smooth operation of the river, lay the source of their future traders' prosperity. Many eyes were on Reith.

As George walked into his office at 16 Robertson Street for a brisk 8.00 a.m. start that spring morning in 1864, he knew that every capability to which, in all sincerity, he had laid claim in his letter of application for the job was now to be tested to the limit. In that letter he had endeavoured to give a fair account of his training and experience: to claim too much would be as self-defeating as to underestimate his accomplishments. The letter had been a fair one, he concluded, as he climbed the dark staircase to his personal office on the top floor. Out of the window he looked across the street to an empty site, gloomy with neglect. 'No doubt,' murmured George to himself, 'before I'm properly in the saddle here, one of the Trustees will be looking around for another and more glorious site for the head office of the Trust. As if externals such as this had any significance at all.' He sniffed contemptuously. 'Instead, however, my task will be to encourage, or to discourage, as appropriate. The essential task is large enough, without bothering about appearances.'

As he paced up and down his room, he eyed the cumbersome desk already in place. Some papers had been placed on its sweeping surface for his attention – no doubt, he thought, for the forthcoming meeting of Trustees that very morning in two hours' time. Was he apprehensive? As he dismissed that idea, he realized that the river was just in sight if he leaned up against the window, caught back the cumbersome velour curtain, and craned his neck to the right. A view of the river signified, for George, the scale of the task awaiting him and his team. 'There we have it, the river itself and centre of our greatest endeavours. First of all, here is this section of Glasgow Harbour, a grand name for an inadequate resource. We must modernize and extend. It hasn't the capacity to justify the name – even though, as I understand it, it is a port of registration. To have achieved that will have pleased the

Trustees, while I seriously doubt that the harbour has attained the required merit. Everything I see and learn points to lack of berth space and of wharfage likewise. And this harbour is to be the focal point of the operations of this river.'

From this mountain-top experience, George retreated to start a list of the factual information he needed. What, for instance, was the limit on tonnage for the use of the harbour? If it were to emerge that no one knew the answers to this and other detailed questions, the staff under him would need to smarten up their act. A fresh sheet was headed 'Tasks'. First listed here was: 'Have meeting with Chief Engineer arranged.' And then, set within question marks, followed names: John Ure? Andrew Duncan?

Another piece of paper now recorded heavier matters, the management of which he had laid claim to in his letter of application. He now drew a copy of this letter out of his new leather wallet, a present from Jean to cheer him on his way on his first day, and looked it over, wishing to assure himself of its continuing validity, along with its references to the many powerful testimonials which had supported his application. His experience in railway management, he had claimed, was to some extent analogous to those duties which fall to the Manager of the Navigation Trust.

George heaved a sigh of satisfaction. He recalled the time and effort that had gone into the phrasing of the section on engineering, straining, as he had done, after accuracy and the truth, such as would in no way diminish what he must value as the fruits of experience, without offering a reduced picture of his undoubted capabilities in the field. George was not going to be caught out favouring the duties that were challenging and glorious in such a way as to bypass the necessity for a true grasp of detail as underpinning efficiency. His letter concluded with a rotund affirmation of co-operation in the furnishing of any more information that might be needed, and an assurance of his ambition 'to conduct the business of the Trust with the firmness and courtesy which contribute so much to secure confidence and command success'. After which 'he had the honour to be, Gentlemen, Your most obedient Servant, (signed) George Reith'.

The Trust, he had learned, had borrowing powers of more than one and a half million pounds. The terrain for which it had responsibility stretched from Glasgow Harbour to the mouth of the River Kelvin, on both banks of the Clyde. 'Not nearly enough!' he growled to himself. 'Pathetic, in fact.' New territory was essential to the realization of much of the development of further quay frontage, and for the acquisition of land by entrepreneurs ready to open ship-building yards and new graving docks. Here George experienced the thrilling realization that steam ships, screw-propelled rather than paddle driven, iron built rather than wooden, would usher in a new sweep of productivity on the river. There was a searching reality to this dream, which connected in George's mind with his notion of the creativity of the engineering skills of David Napier; those which had made it essential that he depart his original workshop at Camlachie in favour of the more spacious, central accommodation available at Lancefield, close by, below the Broomielaw. Out of this initiative George looked ahead to all those engine sheds and boiler works, foundries and workshops, to the manufacture of shafts and gears, all of which must be properly accommodated.

No sooner had George sat down at his desk than there came a knocking at his door. He shouted 'Come in!', thinking with approval that they were good timekeepers here, it being exactly 9 o'clock. In walked a short, dapper man, much laden with files, stacked up on his arms before him, with further wallets hanging from each shoulder. Laboriously, he unloaded some on to George's desk and looked around for a resting place for the remainder. George, watching in hefty silence, made his first managerial decision: he would have to have this under-secretary replaced with another more at home in the territory of big business and those who carried onerous responsibility. With infuriating naivety, this junior held out his hand and announced that he was Alfred McInnes, secretary to the Clerk to the Board of Trustees, and that he hoped very much that he could be of service to Mr Reith. Mr Reith growled his response, held out a reluctant hand, and continued without pause to instruct this junior at once to remove his obstructive heap from his desk.

George continued to scan the papers placed before him for his immediate attention, unimpressed by McInnes' attempts to convey the impression of diligence and efficiency. Later, George Reith, possessed of a soft heart as well as fierce irascibility, relented in favour of firm instructions to Angus Turner, Clerk to the Board, to look to the proper training of juniors in the business; they, after all, were at times called upon to act as its public face. Amateurism such as he had recently experienced damaged the reputation of the business.

The hapless junior could have had no idea what he had sparked, or that his own dismissal was in George's mind. Now George was instructing him to find Mr Angus Turner. Alfred McInnes scuttled out of the room, sensible that all was by no means well, presumably because the boss didn't like things on his desk – a policy he had thought likely to be convenient to the senior man, whom he had so wanted to please.

Shortly, the Clerk to the Board, Angus Turner, knocked on Mr Reith's door and was bidden to enter. He found a hand already outstretched, accompanied not so much by a smile as by a certain relaxation of the furrowed features and the piercing look. The Clerk to the Board had made himself familiar

with the man's reputation, and retained an impassive counte-
nance of his own.

Of all the matters needing the attention of the Board, it had
been agreed at its most recent meeting that the most urgent
was the extension of the docking facilities at the Broomielaw,
Glasgow Harbour. 'After all,' added Angus Turner, unneces-
sarily as he quickly found out, 'we are in severe competition
with the harbours of Leith, Liverpool, Bristol and —'

'Never mind those others,' said George, briskly. 'Here we
stick to the subject. What are the impediments to what we
currently offer, and the range of the solutions that are within
our sights? These, I understand, are the matter of our discussion later this morning.'

The Clerk agreed this to be the case and responded expertly
with the information that he was expected to have at his finger-
tips. 'Currently, ships are needing to berth as many as five deep;
we have insufficient quays. Our harbour is too congested for
the efficient movement of goods. We have established that
the building of further roadways, given the number in place
already, is inappropriate. In addition, there are the river steamers, whose business with sightseers is lucrative for us, although
it is becoming precarious due to the effects of the untreated
sewage through which they have to make their way.'

'Never mind that for the time being. Stick to the outstanding need for more accommodation,' said George peremptorily,
himself fixed on his preference for single-theme exchanges. He
had yet to learn that some subject areas do not admit such
treatment – least of all the Clyde, a watercourse dependent
on the feed from its tributaries. George needed to adapt, from
now on, to concomitant tributaries of thought.

'We have now a marked increase in the number of merchant vessels using our facilities,' said the Clerk to the Board.
'But, as you will appreciate, problems follow in unloading

and transporting goods: the congestion at the quayside is as grave as that of the anchorage itself.'

'Ah,' responded George, this time largely to himself, 'the implications include that remit of ours to work for the enhancement of the prosperity of Glasgow and the West of Scotland.'

Angus continued: 'In relation to the interests of the Trust itself, we ourselves benefit from the payment of rates and dues which are calculated on the basis of registered tonnage. The Act of 1809, in terms of what was then the River Improvement Trust, required the enlargement of Glasgow Harbour and its quays, along with the deepening of the river to a minimum of nine feet at least.' Angus Turner was rehearsing some of the conditions under which Glasgow Harbour operated as an anchorage, for the benefit of the new General Manager.

'What is the maximum depth at present?' asked George.

'As a result of the work of the dredgers,' said Angus, 'it is now twelve feet.'

'I see. Has that enlarged our capacity?' came back the relentless question.

'It means chiefly that we have been able to increase our uptake of passengers as well as goods. For passengers, there are valuable connections with Scottish coastal towns such as Largs, Ayr and Campbeltown and we also offer services to Belfast and to Liverpool. These, of course, are all steam-powered vessels of greater tonnage. We have much to appreciate in the work of Mr Charles Randolph, one of our Trustees. He and his partner John Elder have achieved much in their Engine Works – which is now translated to their company – through their development of steam.'

Here George refrained from responding that he knew more of this activity than his informant was aware. He was noticing that each topic interlocked with another; that Angus was not being muddle-headed in the connections that he was making. The story of the invention of the tug was a good example. A Mr Cochrane instituted a service for the rapid conveyance of luggage, letters and varieties of cargo between Glasgow and Greenock. His two steam-powered vessels were able to offer tows to barges and lighters, enabling goods and raw materials to be moved more rapidly, and reducing the tendency of barges to occupy valuable space. As a result someone had had the brilliant idea of a vessel of at least 40 horse power that could act as a tug. The *Samson* was built in Dumbarton. It had a significant future, especially in relation to the movement downstream of newly constructed hulls to their fitting-out basins.

'I trust, sir,' Turner said, 'that I do not appear to digress from the importance of today's topic: the urgency for the enlargement of Glasgow Harbour, and a resolution as to how best this might be achieved.' For Mr Reith and Mr Turner to work together, there must be an understanding as to the best treatment of a multiplicity of sub-themes in favour of the larger truth.

'I understand,' said George, 'that this subject will have occupied the minds of the Trustees on previous occasions and, likewise, the many interconnecting themes. Can you tell me, broadly speaking, whether this is an issue that gives rise to contentions among the Trustees, or whether, in your view, with careful steering, we may reach agreement as to the way ahead?'

Angus replied carefully, well aware that some of the minds, out of a personal style of their own, tended to take a pride in taking up a contrary position and holding on to it.

'How does our Chief Engineer stand in relation to the many solutions?' enquired George. 'I have yet to meet Mr Andrew Duncan'

Angus was quick enough to pick up on a hint and announce action on it. 'I will get a message to Mr Duncan please to attend on you here a quarter of an hour before we are due to meet at eleven o'clock,' he said.

George nodded approval.

With the first syllable that was uttered, Andrew Duncan and George Reith recognized each other as fellow countrymen. Duncan hailed from Morayshire and had gained a local reputation for his work on the many small east coast fishing harbours. Now his word on the options available for the enlargement of Glasgow Harbour carried weight. George greeted him with cordiality, although sensible that here was a man with diminished energy. Duncan seemed far from well. George was more gentle with him than was his custom. He would, he said, appreciate a resumé by Mr Duncan of the opportunities and the drawbacks attaching to the choices available to them at present.

Andrew Duncan spoke about nearby Stobcross itself. As expected, he spoke tactfully of the inconveniently located Barclay Curle yard, from which followed the necessity to shift cargoes by horse and cart. More roads were inadvisable; there was, he added, the real possibility that the Edinburgh to Glasgow Railway had the land adjacent earmarked for railway extension. They needed, apparently, a station there to connect with their Helensburgh line.

Duncan continued, explaining that there was the question of compulsory purchase by the Trustees of Barclay Curle. George questioned whether such a route would be likely to find favour with the Trustees. Relieved, Andrew Duncan agreed, and outlined suggestions made by his predecessor, John Ure, Chief Engineer from 1853 to 1858, that new quays, off channel, be built. They would be best sited at both Stobcross and Windmillcroft, the latter upstream from Stobcross on the south bank. Such quays would be designed either as open basins, subject to tidal activity, or as enclosed wet docks, equipped with gates – ideas favoured by John Ure.

George specifically wanted to know Mr Duncan's preference. It would carry weight with the Board. Andrew Duncan was clearly pleased, but honest enough to insist on including the possible construction of off-stream docks, attaching to existing anchorages. He made it clear that in his opinion the best option lay on the opposite bank at Windmillcroft. With George Reith's approval he wished to recommend that open tidal basins be introduced – as opposed to the enclosed wet dock, with all the added expense of gates. An enclosed dock would have the advantage of a vessel being kept continuously afloat, but the gates could be opened at high water only, after which there was a risk of grounding in the lower reaches where the depth was regularly little more than four feet.

The task of creating a seating plan of the Trustees was accomplished for George by Angus Turner shortly before the unmistakable sound of the arrival of a carriage, drawn by significantly more than two horses, and the solemn escorting of the distinguished Chair of the meeting, in the person of the City's Lord Provost, to his place. Around the table were arranged the magistrates and the councillors, the ship owners, the representatives of the Chamber of Commerce and of the Trades' House, and those representing the ratepayers.

In a well-tuned utterance, the more effective for its brevity, the Lord Provost Chair of the Board of Trustees welcomed Mr Reith to his new position, a role which combined the challenges of opportunity interwoven with those of responsibility. He went on to assure the company that he had no doubt that they all would, from now on, continue to enjoy the felicity of their appointment of Mr Reith to the task – a decision which they all so heartily supported.

The Chair's speech completed and received with applause, George rose to his feet with a show of great dignity and, with the permission of the Chair, made his opening remarks. He managed to engage with each expectant look from around the table by way of his gimlet glare, delivered from his distinguished height. A scene of this nature was readily picked up and imitated by the grandson that was later to be his: John Reith of the BBC.

George's statement made clear the honour that he felt he had received from them, each and every one, in their acceptance of his application for the job. He assured them that he had studied the matters of their recent meetings. And following a most valuable briefing by Mr Angus Turner and by Mr Andrew Duncan also, he was pleased to find that the task of this, their first meeting as a Board, was the enlargement of the accommodation to be made available here at Glasgow Harbour. Now, he felt sure, the meeting would wish to hear the results of the study which Mr Duncan had made of the opportunities identified by him as areas for possible development, along with the constraints attaching. George did not waste the Committee's time with elegant niceties about the tasks ahead of them, but bowed to the Lord Provost to indicate that it was now on his invitation that Mr Duncan might make his statement.

The site offering the least opportunity, said the Chief Engineer, was Stobcross itself, next to which they were currently stationed. He did not omit the very real hazard attached to the apparent aim of the Edinburgh and Glasgow Railway Company to acquire land adjacent to the Stobcross docks, which, if the Trust were to proceed with this as one of their significant options, whether now or in the future, would effectively cancel any further progress. They needed, he advised, to look well into the future also.

Andrew Duncan concluded with so expert and convincing a recommendation of the scheme for Windmillcroft, on the south bank – with its reliance on one or more tidal basins – that the Board were able to vote in favour of that option. The sense of relief in the meeting was palpable. Several members made a point of congratulating Andrew Duncan on the convincing expertise of his presentation, remarking that never, in their experience as a Trustee, had a unanimous conclusion been so readily reached. Others attributed this happy outcome to George, who brushed it aside, remarking that it had been his good fortune to have experienced at his initial meeting so able a statement as that made by Mr Duncan, whom he now wished to congratulate.

As George did so, shaking him warmly by the hand, he noticed that the engineer seemed quite spent; his effort at sharing his conviction with the Board had cost him dear. The meeting now being concluded, George and his engineer went back to George's office with George counselling Andrew Duncan to return home at once; to take a cab, charge it up to the Trust, and to take a good rest. He had offered the Trust no mean service that day, he concluded.

Andrew Duncan's tasks for the Clyde Navigation Trust were indeed over. Debility prevented all further exertions; in all too short a time he must relinquish his post as its Chief Engineer.

12

The Man of Feeling

One evening some months later, wearied from a day in the office, George awarded himself a walk along the river, making his way along its north bank, bypassing the Barclay Curle yard and weaving his way across the roadways that encircle the dock. 'I wonder how Govan Tommy is managing his lameness with his broom handle,' he thought. Without difficulty, George would pass through Tod and Macgregor's yard, and then probably reach open country, from where he might look across to Govan. That was somewhere he felt he needed to revisit, given the place it had had in his formative first impressions of Glasgow, and of the task that awaited him.

Here at Tod and Macgregor's yard, he was at once recognized by the workers. George valued exchanges with them. He made it clear to them, somewhat pompously, that he depended on their diligence and expertise. The language he used was different from that familiar to the men. But they understood one another nevertheless. He found himself envying them the thrill that was rightly theirs when their ships were launched. 'The birth,' said he, working to choke back a lump of emotion a great new ship gliding down the runway.

'Aye,' said one sceptical worker, making it his task to counter what he felt was the absurdity of a tough man's emotion when the reality was hard, grinding work, often in bitter weather. The missus and the bairns at home, what about them? And would the yard get another order?

George, well used to tough belligerence such as this, told the increasing group of listeners that they were to remember that the Clyde Navigation Trust was there to fight for their livelihood and for more orders for the yards. Now, he said, he was pleased to meet them, and he made clear his readiness to listen to their views, even though he called a halt as soon as he suspected criticism of their employers, Mr Macgregor or Mr Tod, about to surface.

In response to his request a group led him to the exit from the yard which readily connected with what remained of the footpath leading westwards.

'Aye,' came a new voice, 'along there you'll find a wee guy scribbling away at his easel. He calls himself William Crimea Simpson. He came to these shores as a wee lad, he says. But . . .' – here the voice trailed away in uncertainty – 'ah did nae ken am sure.'

George thanked them; as he turned away a small cheer went up, and he returned their greeting in a wave.

George knew that he must never lose touch with the workforce, to whichever yard they belonged. Everything depended on their morale and on understanding all round. A new realization struck him: these men were, so to speak, the aristocrats of the labouring classes of Glasgow. Ships were to become the symbol of Glasgow, the expression of its industrial pride. His thoughts flew on: ships were, he thought wildly, its glory and its virtue. The extent of his task knew few boundaries. George Reith was not to be found forever behind his desk, blazing fire at his back, attentive staff scurrying in and out, and status-conscious persons bowed in his presence.

But then, also, he must never let up on the task and the role of the Navigation Trust had to be recognized and understood by all its office bearers – from annoying functionaries like Alfred McInnes to, particularly, the Clerk to the Board, Angus Turner. About the latter he realized that he retained as yet an open mind. George knew that he needed to maintain a vision for the future while tackling the management of the main issues such as purification of the river and providing accommodation for the many ancillary industries. It was his task to provide leadership to both the Board and to the paid staff. Now, he realized with some conviction, commitment to the front-line workers themselves was vital – although, of course, always with the full consent, if not the actual presence, of their managers. And then, he must not lose sight of the need for constant attention to the huge and risky sums that were called for in financial management.

Slightly shaken by the heights encompassed by his role, he found himself taking a look back at his family in Stonehaven. With the exception of his brother David, he did wonder, in all modesty, from where his own insistent drive and these aptitudes had come. His parents, Mary and Alexander Reith, were sorry figures, with their drink and everything that followed from it. Had that, he wondered, induced in him a resolve to break out and away from the constrictions offered by the tollhouse? In addition he had no doubt about the lasting effect of those all-too-brief encounters with those leading figures in engineering: Thomas Telford and Robert Stevenson. These events and influences had, he knew, amounted in him to the experience of an ignited flame; directives which were as clear and persuasive as his resolve to pursue them with his utmost effort.

Now his train of thought was quite stopped. It was unusual, surely, in this area and at this evening hour, with its accompanying chill, to come upon a seated figure, intent on some task before him. And then – 'Of course,' thought George to himself, 'he is a painter wishing to record this idyllic rural scene, before it all disappears under the machinations of the Navigation Trust.' From time to time George encountered the clash between the old and the emerging new – these things continued to carry their discomforts, and their revelations too. Just now, he purposely stepped on snapping twigs and waded through troughs of last autumn's leaves in order not to overtake with fright this artist at work.

As intended, when he drew alongside the easel he could do so without startling the man and the delicacy of his work with brush and palette. He was sorry to interrupt, he said, but he had come to enjoy the experience of this so significant picture of the Water Row. The old houses of Govan leaned together as though to prop one another up as they accompanied the route to the water's edge; 'And there,' he exclaimed 'I see you have the Ferry Bote Inn!'

George said again, how sorry he was to interrupt, but he would be glad to know who it was he now had the honour to meet.

The painter smiled up gently; he said he was William Simpson, and that his delight was to record scenes such as this attaching 'to this great river of ours. I am working colour, as I see it, into a sketch I did twenty years ago.'

George introduced himself, reckoning to himself that Mr Simpson was by only a few years his junior.

'Ah,' said Mr Simpson, connecting to George without a trace of rancour his role in imposing industry onto this rural retreat, 'before long we will experience the results of your labours, the tentacles of industry will continue to extend their grip over this very spot where you and I can now savour its rustic charm.' He noted how the iron industry had been developing in the area for 80 years. Coal and ironstone were locally available from Muirkirk, to the south of Glasgow, and steam power had been applied to furnaces, forges and mills. 'But,' Simpson added hastily, 'I by no means intend to speak critically of your magnificent aspirations, all of which will benefit our ancient city and its people, and this the land we love.'

'Thank you,' said George. 'You are a man of great generosity. And you have come here, no doubt, to capture the ancient beauties of this spot before they are overtaken by the advances of technology?' They were in accord that no one would ever remove the Doomster Hill, or the great sarcophagus within the church, or the ancient hog-back stones and the wealth of their narrative, yet to be deciphered.

Simpson remarked on the Old Govan Church too, with the quiet of its most graceful steeple, symbol of the aspirations of the life fulfilled, and supposed that no one would consider that another church should replace it.

George decided not to disturb the calm of their exchange with intrusive facts. Instead, picking up on a wealth of experience that was emerging from this thoughtful man's every utterance, he enquired about other areas where he had possibly set up his easel.

The reply was startling. 'I am a war artist,' said William Simpson; 'they call me "William *Crimea* Simpson", since I worked in the Crimea for some years, until I begged a break under the heading of sick leave. I published the results of my work as War Artist back here in 1855 under the title *The Seat of the War in the East*. To recover I needed to return to the scenes of my youth – my father was a marine engineer, and I was brought up near here. I love it as it is, and I needed to record it before change came upon it.

'But,' he added, 'I do repeat that in no way do I criticise the essential work that you do; after all, it's that insistence which had in part brought me back to this spot. You see, there are many of us artists. You will be familiar with the work of John Knox, in which he vividly captures the progress of our first steam-powered ship up the Clyde, the others, with their gracious sails, clustering around, seemingly out of curiosity. John is long dead now,' added William sadly.

'Ah, yes,' said George, pleased to be able to contribute a little of his own experience in this new field. He had indeed seen Knox's picture, and had been much taken with the narrative it provided. 'A funny lash-up of a vessel she was, the *Comet*, the work of a hotelier wishing to promote his wife's business,' said he, disparagingly. 'But no, in fact, the invention of that ship set in motion one of the great imperatives of our present time: the development of steam as a reliable power source. Mr Knox's painting points the way to a very bright future.'

'Have you met Mr Robert Napier?' enquired William Simpson.

George at once replied, 'That is a task to which I look forward very much. Hardly can I turn around than there are more signs of his visionary work; of his inventions, both in technology and, more significantly, in industrial relations. I long to sit at his feet to learn about my job, and about the resonances of that ringing term "Clydebuilt" for which he was the inspiration. We have much to live up to.'

'I hope,' William continued on a note of gentle solicitude, 'that you do not find the responsibilities of your job apt to distance you from good friends and the encouragement of those who have an understanding of the responsibilities you carry.' A little stiffened from remaining seated at his task too long, William rose, and he and George shook hands cordially.

George assured his new friend that he was much blessed in that his wife had moved from her native Aberdeenshire to join him in Glasgow, where she would delight to fill her house with guests. He did not expect a lonely life. With that he started out again on the riverside path, his mind filled with the recollection of their exchange.

At 16 Queen's Crescent, the small spare bedroom on the top floor was, for the time being, occupied by his son George who was working in the Wynds of Glasgow off the High Street and into the Saltmarket. His appointment to this Free Church charge had come about through the influence of Dr Thomas Chalmers, that great leader of the momentous Disruption within the Church.

Tonight, George returned refreshed from his outdoor walk and meeting with William Simpson, and proposed that he and his son go to hear a public lecture to be given that night by Lord Kelvin, the genius Professor of Mathematics and Natural Philosophy at Glasgow University. George junior enthusiastically agreed. After tea, the pair of them marched with determined step towards Gilmorehill, the new campus. Their knowledge of this man Kelvin, they admitted to one another, was slight; the best they could do was to piece together their respective fragments. Lord Kelvin, now aged roughly 40, had come from Belfast as plain William Thomson when his father had assumed the Chair of Mathematics in Glasgow.

They eventually found the lecture hall for that evening – the task made harder because the current building programme required many detours which were poorly signed. They found a queue already forming, and during their wait before Lord Kelvin began, father and son took advantage of their time together.

George senior had questions for his minister son about living conditions in the High Street. He had heard that the demolition of some of the more insanitary buildings had been considered, and wondered what would happen to those thus evicted.

George junior, in response, explained that the City Improvement Trust was singling out the priorities for demolition and was having the buildings recorded in photographic form. Thomas Annan, one of the world's earliest photographers, would shortly be starting work on his commission with the condemned buildings. It was to be called 'The Old Closes and Streets of Glasgow'. 'This is a most far-sighted commission by the Improvement Trust,' George junior said, 'to ensure that future generations can understand a little of how people once lived here.'

'And so, where do the evicted families go?' was his father's pertinent question. 'And, anyway – what is photography?'

'I'm not too sure about your second question, Father,' replied George, 'except that a photograph is a picture resulting from a chemical acting in light on sensitive material of some kind. Given the right conditions it will, I understand, reproduce a scene with stunning accuracy. That is where the City Improvement Trust is being so far-sighted; although much more so by the simultaneous programme for the building of new accommodation. You can see rows of new substantial buildings in the Gorbals. The stone from which these handsome tenement buildings are constructed is mostly local but there are also some builidings constructed from red sandstone that has been carted all the way up from Dumfriesshire. The great asset offered by these buildings is that, on each landing, there is a communal water closet, the people having been denied any such facility all their days.'

George senior conceded that these were indeed all changes for the better. By now, it was clear that it was time to hush – they had taken their seats and the lecturer was about to be introduced.

An hour later, they were endeavouring to keep up with the lecture using their rather rudimentary understanding of physics. They were careful, all the same, to attribute the difficulty to their own newness to the field rather than to any obscurity on the part of the lecturer. Kelvin had left them in no doubt as to his highly developed aptitude for communication and engagement with an audience – who made no pretence of familiarity with his subject.

Next morning, back in the office, George Reith found himself much stimulated by the recollection of the lecture. Both content and delivery impressed him and he felt justifiably proud by the company of his son.

At his desk he found, as he had requested, the original of the report submitted to the city magistrates by one John Golborne, consisting of his proposal to the City for the improvement of the overall depth of the river. Oddly, now, September 1868, it was almost exactly 100 years since the publication of the report. George found that it applied chiefly to the lower reaches of the river. He was aware that a succession of studies and reports had been prepared: there were those by Thomas Telford, John Rennie and John Smeaton also. But this one, drawn up against a background of experience of English rivers with similar tendencies to silt up, had rightly caught the attention of the magistrates, and despite its age it was still regarded as the authoritative work. Impressed by the status of this ageing document, with its ragged edges, discoloured paper, and all-too-human crossings out, the General Manager was clear that it was the definitive study, with which he needed to be thoroughly familiar. Even at that time the outstanding problem that had faced Glasgow was the persistent silting up of the river, and therefore the diminishing usefulness to the City of Port Glasgow itself.

John Golborne's proposals were almost misleadingly simple. He had noted that the sides of the river were formed of softer material than that which formed the river bed. Thus the current tended to erode the sides, causing the river to gain in breadth what it was wanting in depth. His aim was to quicken the current of the river by reducing its width and, thereby, increasing its speed. Travelling in a narrower channel, the river itself would act on its sandy bed and become self-scouring. For the magistrates' consideration, Mr Golborne offered the building of a series of projecting jetties or dykes, set at right angles to the flow and at a regular distance apart. The resulting channel would release in the river a new velocity, so that it would carry its silt downstream to the open estuary and the sea, where it would be abandoned without further obstruction to the passageway of the river. These proposals would solve the problem and meet the requirements of the City. His dykes would be built all the way from downstream Dumbuck into Glasgow itself. Later, they would be followed by what he called a 'training wall', the purpose of the latter being to prevent the accumulation of silt and grit in-between the dykes. Mr Golborne ended his recommendation with his humble conclusion that 'the River Clyde may be deepened so as to have four feet, or perhaps five feet depth up to the Broomielaw'.

John Golborne received his fee of £85, and was informed of the magistrates' decision that they must implement his report without delay. They commissioned him, as was the custom of the time, to execute the carrying out of the plan with his own labour squad and equipment: he was to provide all possible machines, material and manpower needed, and to be in personal attendance at least six months of every year.

Golborne had calculated that even if the costs were to exceed £10,000, the benefits would greatly outrun the cost. His aim was to attain a minimum highwater depth of seven feet. For £11,000 he as contractor undertook to create that seven foot depth at every neap or high tide.

The work started in September 1771. The activity was immense. Quarries were opened to provide foundations for the jetties; labourers and craftsmen camped along the shores. By the end of 1772, 100 jetties had been completed bringing about a consistent depth of five feet throughout.

Supplementary to his scheme, Golborne advised what he called spoon dredgers to assist in the removal of persisting shoals and reefs. This traditional method amounted to no more than an iron or wooden spoon mounted on the end of a long pole, with various ways found to introduce the lever effect. Later followed the more elaborate dredging plough: this in many ways worked in the style of a land plough, bringing up, it was claimed, half a ton of gravel each time and depositing it on the bank.

The Golborne plan was early implemented. Now, it seemed to George Reith that the effectiveness of it might well not have dated by much in the interval, given the energy of the river in action over that long period of time. He had a question for Angus Turner: 'So – what happened in the meantime that the river should so deteriorate, both as to depth and as to the quality of the water?'

Turner gave Reith a report of the changes and improvements made to the jetty system. 'Overall,' said Turner, 'however, the task of the dredgers was found to be essential and of a continuing nature.'

George considered this and noted the need to study, and possibly invent, further designs for more powerful dredgers. A meeting with the Chief Engineer took place and Andrew Duncan brought with him two completed dredger designs. With some zest, George Reith could enter into debate on the firm basis of his own background in engineering. In due course, two new models were costed and approved by the Board and, working in support of the Golborne plans, steadily increased the consistent navigability of the river.

The success of the Trustees in the welcome management of the river for the benefit of merchant shipping so invigorated the Glasgow magistrates as to open the way, in George's judgement, to gaining support for the urgent need for action on the pollution of the river.

Some of the merchant members of the Navigation Board were decidedly opposed to the raising of the issue, assured, they believed, of an outcome of no account whatever. 'Anyway,' they concluded, 'it's simply not within our province to try to take action on the city's sewerage.'

George Reith swept the boardroom with a penetrating look and, with unhurried and ominous speech, gave his differing point of view. 'It is not for us, in the withdrawn circumstances and the comfort of this room to condemn our own men, our employees, to perform the essential work of the dredgers in circumstances which are too noxious even to consider. Gentlemen, our task, our responsibility, is more than to support them in their work: it is to enable them to carry out their task to the best of their ability, without danger to their health or that of their families, and in the knowledge that they have the undivided support of this boardroom. With our men we share the responsibility to carry out the scouring of the river, and the retaining of her navigable depth. I cannot believe that any one of us would wish to withdraw from the task we share to persuade the City of the urgent need to introduce sewage treatment plants at intervals within reach of the river.' George sat down heavily, awaiting the reaction.

When it came, from more than one quarter of the room, it was with the voice of social concern, not only for those who toiled on or in the vicinity of the river, but also for those whose ships came alongside her wharfage to offload merchandise.

'And then,' came another voice, 'what about the crews of the river steamers? After which,' the voice continued expansively, 'we need look no further than to the Saltmarket and to the High Street to gain an awareness of the lives of those people whose children have been condemned to drink this filthy water and to carry out such ablutions as they could in its state of contamination.'

Fellow Trustees would be aware, concluded another voice, that typhus was again taking its toll.

Even if the living conditions of the population were not strictly speaking within their remit, many found that Mr Reith's arguments, in terms of the multitudes of employees, and their responsibilities for their welfare, unanswerable. Thus it was agreed that the twin claims on the resources of the Trust were for the construction of the two dredgers as recommended by the Chief Engineer, and the exercise of time and persuasion in relation to management by the City of 'intercepting sewers' leading downriver to outfalls.

Sensibly, George Reith kept his silence throughout the contributions to the argument. He knew persuasion from within was very much more significant. His own arguments might always run the risk of the backlash of dissent.

If Mr Reith felt that sense and good judgement had at last prevailed, he could feel little more than a despondent rage at events around the manoeuvres of the Edinburgh and Glasgow Railway Company. He had, he believed, done everything possible to convince his staff that the matter – the risk, indeed – of the Railway Company proceeding with their designs to appropriate a stretch of land at Stobcross, on which the Trust also had serious designs, must always be kept to the forefront of minds and agendas. Now, in the context of the urgent need of the Trust for more land, the Railway Company had been quicker off the mark. The land that they needed to accommodate a new station for their Helensburgh line was conveniently to be had at Stobcross. Had they been able to snatch the prized territory from under the Trust's nose?

George Reith summoned Angus Turner. 'Have you,' the question came in ominous tones, 'attended to the papers associated with the application by the railway for the territory in question?' Not pausing for an answer, Reith continued, 'Did not the minutes of the Trustees' meeting, in which Andrew Duncan expounded the risk now attaching to this railway and their interest in the territory in question clearly indicate this matter demanded action – did you not attend to the matter in such a way as to bring it to my attention, and thus to that of the Board?'

Reith was furious; Turner had nowhere to go. He had, indeed, been remiss on all these points – his only excuse being his attention to the expansion of Glasgow Harbour in the manner recommended by Mr Duncan, to proceed at Windmillcroft.

'That is no excuse,' exploded Reith. 'If I cannot trust my senior staff to be consistently up to date with major threats of this nature, we betray the trust placed in us by our Trustees, all of whom are senior figures who have neither the time nor the patience to waste on amateur fumbling of this kind. What do you say to this? You are perhaps overtaxed by your responsibilities as they currently exist.'

This in turn angered Mr Turner, who redirected the responsibility for this lapse towards George himself: the two men were at loggerheads.

George knew that if Turner were to resign as a result, the loss would by no means be irreparable. To the retreating form of the hapless Turner he threw out a question: was the railway company likely to be in debt?

Turner's answer was addressed mainly to the door post. 'That is likely,' he said. 'Anyway,' he added, visited by another surge of anger, 'it was agreed that the Stobcross scheme be put on hold in favour of Duncan's Windmillcroft plan.'

George didn't bother to reply, his mind busy on a scheme by which they might outwit the railway. Earlier that year the railway company had submitted a bill to Parliament seeking permission to construct their branch line to Helensburgh for both goods and passengers. The bill was presented to the Trustees of the Clyde Navigation Trust for comment, but they were so preoccupied with their own affairs that they offered no comment. Thus it was with horror that Reith realized that the ground that the railway proposed to develop was the same as they had had in their sights to enlarge the basin at Stobcross. With the bill passed, the development of the basin had now become almost an impossibility.

Reith's experience of the law, however, came to his aid. Under the terms of the Act, the railway was bound to complete the development within nine years of approval obtained, or the powers would lapse, and the money run out. He was able to find out that the railway company needed more money to complete the project within the time allocated. And they had no hope of raising it. George Reith's ingenious solution was to offer them a loan of £150,000 repayable over five years on condition that the railway agreed to sell to the Trustees the land needed for the larger basin. In return, the Board would ensure that an equivalent stretch of land, such as the railway needed, was made available to them for sidings to serve the quays. This ingenious solution was to the advantage of the Trust, since their need for space for the movement of merchandise was outstanding. The offer was accepted and it was in 1870 that the construction of a 700-foot-wide basin at Stobcross was begun.

13

Artists and Craftsmen: The Napier Cousins

George Reith was not so leathery as not to experience some reaction as a result of the recent fallings from grace. These troubles had arisen out of his leadership, he felt, as well as from the performance of senior staff, for which he also took responsibility. In fact, stern moralist that he was, and with scope and determination to match, he took it upon himself to tackle the inevitable Corrievrechan of business. Jean, his wife, picked up on his disquiet: 'You often mention to me the reputation of this man Robert Napier. Even though, as I understand, he is now retired, might you not find that he has experience to share with you, that he too has come through difficult times? Maybe from his example you could see new reflections on what you have achieved, and what opportunities could be ahead?

George was impressed by his wife's concern, as well as astonished at her perception, not having realized that he had become so transparent to his mood. She was right: he must act, and along the lines she suggested. Robert Napier, now retired, lived at Shandon; not the easiest place to reach.

He must accustom himself to a longish journey, most of which could be by river steamer, and the rest in a hired cab.

As he disembarked, however, he saw a man step forward at the foot of the gangway.

'Mr Reith?' he said courteously. 'I'm Davie. Mr Napier sent me to meet you and take you to his house.'

'That is kind of him,' murmured George, gratefully accepting this gracious welcome.

The driver led George up to the gig, loaded on his bag for him and the passenger climbed aboard. Davie now dismissed the small boy who had been waiting around in hope of a horse's head to be held in exchange for a coin or two. The little fellow got his pay and rushed off to join his friends.

In no time they had bowled up the hill to the gracious house built by Robert and his wife for their retirement. The driver now, with a word to his horse, sprang up the steps to pull at the bell, and returned to carry up George's bag. And so George fetched up at that front door and turned round to admire the view to the south and to the east up the river. He understood how it was that Robert Napier, with his strenuous life arising out of the situation and potential of that waterway, must, in his retirement, continue his watching brief over it.

The door was opened. There he was, with hand held out in welcome; and there, smiling behind him, was his wife. She escorted George to his room, and invited him, when he was ready, to join them in the sitting room, which he would find to the left of the front door.

Downstairs, with a glass of wine in his hand, and George with his – good manners insisted, he decided – Robert was congratulating George on the advances of which he had already heard, in his onerous job with the Clyde Navigation Trust. 'I have heard too,' said Robert, managing not to sound conspiratorial, 'that you have persuaded the Trust to take on responsibility for the woeful absence of any form of sewage treatment for the river and for the benefit of those who must earn their living by it. You, sir, must have consummate skills of persuasion to win the agreement of the Board, which after all has a large enough remit as it is.'

'Sir,' responded George, thrown by the liveliness of this man's continuing connection with affairs, 'I must return your tribute to where it belongs; that is, to the magnanimity of the Board members. When it was pointed out to them that it was employees of ours who were thus put at risk, and their families with them, they at once took up the argument for our taking responsibility for the noxious state of the river. Even though, as we know, this outreach is not within the statutes of the Trust. I simply sat back and let them get on with it. And you, sir, I think I detect that you hail from these parts?'

'My father was a blacksmith in Dumbarton,' replied Robert. 'He wanted me to go into the ministry; but I was much influenced by my cousin David, whose yard was originally out at Camlachie. He drew up a new design there for a ship with the capacity to cross the Atlantic. He had something of the artist in him, had David,' said Robert dreamily.

David had written of himself:

I commenced, I think about the year 1818, to build a steamer on my own account for the purpose [of crossing the Atlantic], called the *Rob Roy*. I recollect the day, before starting on the first trip from Glasgow to Dublin, Mr Charles MacIntosh, the celebrated chemist and inventor of waterproof cloth, saying we should all be drowned. Nevertheless, we did start and although we encountered a gale from the south west, performed the voyage out and home successfully.

'David,' said his cousin, as he finished reading this piece from a letter, 'had all manner of setbacks and disbelief in his designs. When he handed his model of *Rob Roy* to his shipbuilder, and told him to make a ship in the form which he now held in his hand, the shipbuilder cried out in disbelief. *Rob Roy*, however, was a success. David moved from the limitations of his site at Camlachie, in favour of the new one at Lancefield, on the north bank of the river, downstream a little from Stobcross. I joined him there for a spell. His works there were considerable and, not content with that, he excavated a dock with which to complete the orders that were now pouring into his office. In 1826 he built the first of his two 'leviathans', the *United Kingdom*, which was 160 feet long, with engines of 200 horsepower, and equipped with all manner of inventions. And then, if that were not enough, he designed and built a most quaint horseless conveyance, which when seen making its way along the roads of Cowal, did so to the alarm and curiosity of the populace.

'But then the oft-predicted disaster did strike after all. The *Earl Grey*, another of his amazing constructions, blew up in Greenock harbour, with loss of life as a result. To this day you may find a stone in the graveyard of Paisley Abbey recounting this dreadful tale and naming those who lost their lives. My cousin made his way to London, mortified; he felt he could never again hold up his head on Clydeside. There he and his sons built iron vessels; he was continuing his innovations in his new life.'

Robert offered George a top-up of his glass – which George refused – and told how he had shared ownership of his cousin's Lancefield Works in 1821, before moving to the better sited Vulcan Works at 28 Washington Street, a little further downstream.

'But now,' said Robert, 'Elspeth and I are curious to know what brought you here to the Clyde – apart, that is, from your own reputation for, how shall I say, "getting things done"?'

George hesitated before replying. 'I think I was heavily influenced by some chance encounters. Back in Stonehaven, where I grew up, our harbour was disastrously incommoded by a giant rock at its centre. Our local council seemed unable to act, even though it deprived many an aspiring young man of his livelihood at the herring. Eventually, word got into their thick heads,' said George, more relaxed in this enabling company than he had quite noticed, 'that there was this giant among civil engineers—'

'Robert Stevenson,' broke in Napier with a broad smile.

'Who other?' said George appreciatively. 'At last a harbour inspection by the great man was arranged. I, then in my impressionable youth, learned with great thoroughness the amazing exploits achieved by Stevenson and his sons to foil the disgraceful trade of the wreckers. I found somewhere within myself the resolution that it must be to further such maritime causes that I was to labour on this earth. My meeting with Stevenson was very brief indeed, but this, and his grandson's poem, confirmed my aspirations. You will, I am sure, be familiar with Robert Louis' stirring description of those many lighthouses erected by the family at enormous personal risk, most especially that attached to the Bell – or Inchcape Rock. I even,' said George, embarrassed, 'recall a little of that poem which I found so stirring: how

> a strenuous family dusted from its hands
> The sands of granite and beholding far
> Among the sounding coasts its pyramids
> And tall memorials catch the dying sun.

George now cleared his throat noisily, unsure where to go from here. But Robert Napier, visibly moved, came to his rescue.

'My goodness, George. You and I share a rich inheritance and a living influence. Like you, in my youth, unsure where to go, even though not into the Church, my apprenticeship was served in Edinburgh, of all unlikely places, with the same Mr Stevenson. There I was under the strong impression that I would not get my supper unless I had accurately counted the newly fashioned iron lamp holders adorning the streets of New Town Edinburgh – Edinburgh's ironwork was, after all, the winter mainstay of his business, when even he would listen to advice about the dangers of winter storms at sea. Like you, that experience has stayed with me and done much to shape my subsequent career, even though I moved away from street furniture in iron, feeling that the advances in iron vessels were more exciting.

Hearing a knock on the door Mrs Napier called out 'Come in!'

A young girl came shyly a little distance into the room and addressed her mistress, using a well-rehearsed part: 'Please, ma'am, Cook says to say to you that dinner is ready.' Having delivered her piece this country lassie melted out of sight and sound as fast as possible.

Elspeth smiled indulgently, explaining that she and Robert liked to engage local boys and girls to help them with their house and garden, but that they didn't believe in dressing up the girls with mob cap, frilly apron and other such fripperies, which she believed would only embarrass them further. 'Come through!' she now said to George.

When they were seated, the topic of the common experience of the two men started up again. Now, encouraged by George, Robert spoke again, and as ever with modesty about his achievements.

He had, he said, got himself noticed by a wealthy businessman with a penchant for yacht racing. 'Not, you understand, my scene at all. I had always looked upon this sort of thing as vain and silly, the concern of the idle rich; the workhorses of the river and eventually the ocean-going chaps were my babies, the greater the tonnage the better, with mighty engines to power them. There was the thrill. Anyway,' he continued, 'this Mr Assheton Smith would have me design a yacht with which he could assuredly win the coveted Yacht Club Cup. I was far too sensible a man to give Mr Assheton Smith such an assurance. His *Clarence* nevertheless won, and I was landed with more orders almost than I could cope with. This Mr Assheton Smith, who was a bit of an original, fell upon the idea that I should build him a steam yacht, of all things. I have never been able to resist an opportunity, and so off I went. But I was to receive a warning from Mrs Assheton Smith, conveyed to me by her husband.'

At this point Robert's wife firmly took over. Mrs Assheton Smith, she recounted, was totally opposed to an idea so fantastic as steam-powered vessels. Robert, in her view, was 'the plain man from Clydeside'. He had a lot to overcome. The three had dinner together – 'and next morning Robert got his order!' she concluded triumphantly. 'After that,' she added, turning to her husband, 'I think the openings that came your way were more to your liking?'

'I was lucky,' said Robert, taking up his story, 'given that Whitehall, and the Admiralty with it, exhibited a consistent reluctance to work with Scottish engineers. We were to them, apparently, the riffraff. But – I had just engined the *Bernice* for the East India Company. It was then, I think, that Assheton Smith most likely spoke up for me, especially to the Duke of Wellington and to the Lords of the Admiralty, as well as to the governors of the East India Company. I must have appeared a strange, obscure engineer from the boreal regions north of the River Tweed.'

Later, no less a commentator than George Blake noted 'the nuances of the national and commercial jealousy in the

complicated story of Napier's struggle against London pride
and prejudice for recognition as the greatest shipbuilder of his
time'. Napier never set profit above the perfection of the job.
Often, in the early days, his passion for the sheer goodness
of work lost him money on important contracts. His commission for the East India Company, the *Bernice*, was delivered at a high cost to Napier of £30,000. The *Bernice*'s sister
ship, the *Atlanta*, was built and engined on the Thames and
had lagged behind delivery of the *Bernice* by 18 days. Thus,
through *Bernice* doors were at last opened to Robert Napier.
This was in 1837, when the first Napier steam ships reached
China and Australia.

'And then . . .' said he, looking doubtfully first at George
and then at his wife.

'Don't stop, please,' said George insistently. 'This is thrilling stuff.'

'Very well,' said Robert. 'I hate to appear to glory in the
thrills which have come my way, as a fortunate man indeed.
One Samuel Cunard got in touch, a connection made through
the East India Company. Mr Cunard wrote to me through
his agents in Glasgow, proposing a meeting. This took place
at Lancefield, at the end of which we agreed the building of
new vessels at a cost of £30,000 each. After which I realized
that I had made a mistake: that the design of ship which I
was offering was too small for the task. Each would need to
be lengthened and made more powerful at an extra cost of
£2,000. In the meantime, Cunard was having further meetings in London and the Admiralty and the Treasury declared
themselves to be highly pleased with the size of the boats,
but there remained considerable prejudice on the part of the
English builders. Cunard received several offers of building
services from Liverpool and London, and when he replied
that he had contracted in Scotland, they invariably replied

along the lines of, "You will neither have competent work, nor be complete on time."

'But,' said Robert, closing his copious file on these transactions, 'Mr Cunard's comment was excellent: it was to the effect that the Admiralty agreed with him that the boats would be as good as if built in England.'

'Well,' said George, 'anyone else with a less generous spirit could well have taken exception to that remark.'

'Oh, well,' said Robert, 'I had other things exercising my mind at the time, chiefly that I had not yet been courageous enough to tell Mr Cunard of the need to increase the size of the boats. This time Mr Cunard, initially, would not budge. Nor would he pay up. I was absolutely clear by now that the cargo and the conditions likely to be experienced crossing the Atlantic necessitated increased tonnage and horsepower. We had another meeting in Lancefield, and I undertook to raise the money in Scotland. I have often thought,' he interrupted himself, 'it's not making the mistake that matters – it's the recovering from it. Anyway, people were saying that if that was my conclusion as to size, my word should be attended to. And – do you know' – Robert wheeled round to speak directly to George – 'we got the money, all £270,000 that we needed. The result of this process was that we had established the British and North American Royal Mail Steam Packet Company to finance, build and operate the shipping. Latterly it became the Cunard Company, wholly financed by Glasgow men. Next came our first *Britannia*.'

'Ah,' said George, 'I do believe with Charles Dickens aboard?'

'You are right,' replied his host. 'Nor was he the best of sailors. In his *American Notes* he recounts his most unhappy experience.

'What a tribute that was to the resilience of your ship!' smiled George.

'Yes,' said Robert. 'This was her maiden voyage in 1842. With sixty-three on board she made the crossing in fourteen days. She had an amazing reception in Boston, with booming cannons and hundreds lining the quays. For her many successors, I designed what I hoped would be the distinctive livery of the red Cunard funnel, its black top and black lines on the flanges. After *Britannia* we built three more ships for the transatlantic service, each this time averaging a "nominal horse power", as they called it, of 420 nhp.'

'Then, I think, if I am right,' came in George, 'you went on to build the Navy's first three hulls. Was it then that you transferred building engines from Lancefield to the new site in Govan West?'

'Yes,' replied Robert, 'and we were at last recognized and accepted by Whitehall. Then there was an episode of which, in all honesty, I am not proud. I produced a vessel capable of eighteen knots. There opened up for us shipbuilders a rich market in the Americas. The Northern states were led by Abraham Lincoln in his campaign against the slave trade on which they in the South depended. Lincoln's policy was to starve the Southerners of food and materials. The slaughter of men in that war was truly terrible. No price was too high for the Southerners for suitable ships that could dodge the Northern Navy, able to unload supplies under cover of darkness. Rich Southern buyers appeared on the Clyde to buy shallow draft, fast ships that would avoid the Northern blockade.

'We are talking, of course, of the American Civil War, in which the Union in the North blocked the Confederacy of the Southern States. More and more yards were building for this lucrative purpose, seeing their ships putting out to sea from the Clyde in order to deliver arms and luxuries into the Southern States – and to transport cotton out in their fast steamers from the beleaguered Southern ports. The profits to be made for those prepared to take the risk were huge. The trick was to make the three-day ocean crossing from Bermuda or Nassau, keeping to the inland shores; and then to sneak up one of the channels of the few Confederate-held ports during the night. If discovered their speed would enable them to escape, charging through the lines of the blockading Federal gunboats to gain the protection of a Confederate coastal battery. My *Neptune*,' he couldn't help adding, 'could nip by like a bird. I don't deny I made money on her. But this was the point at which Elspeth and I decided I should retire. I should like to have done so without what I believe was a mistaken policy on my part; I was becoming a war profiteer. But I was old and tired; it was time to hand over to others.'

George neither agreed nor disagreed. Instead he was conscious that Robert had given of his energy unstintingly that evening; now, as his wife was saying, it was time to retire, this time up the stairs.

That Robert was an outstandingly fine man, George could not deny. Next morning very quietly, before Robert was down, Elspeth put before George a letter from a tough Controller of the Navy:

> May God bless you, my dear old friend. One of the few bright spots in my official career is that it has again brought me into relations with you, and made me know still better than of old all that was valuable, excellent and sterling in your honoured self.

George was much touched that she should want him to see this letter. As he handed it back to her, she explained that

Robert's policy with regard to naval cadets, and indeed to officers also, was to take them into his shops in order to instruct them in his methods. 'Often,' she said, 'we would have them back here for the weekend; Robert had no trade secrets. They used to tell me that the certificates he handed out to them were among their most treasured possessions.'

14

A Life Well Spent

Now, in 1883, relations between the General Manager and his Principal Clerk had improved to the extent that the latter no longer felt it necessary to await the command to enter Mr Reith's room, following decisive knocking. Rather, he might combine both actions and precipitate himself in at greater speed. This particular morning he was already speaking as he entered.

'There's been an accident, a failed launch.'

'Where?' returned George.

'Stephens Linthouse. The *Daphne*. The yard was thrown by the shortage of time to complete an order for the Laird Line before the Glasgow Fair holidays. It seems,' said Angus Turner, 'that haste spelled disaster.'

The engines were installed in the hull, but not the boilers ahead of the launch. Worst of all, still at work within the hull was a squad of workers. The story that had reached the office was that the *Daphne* took to the water perfectly. And then – horror – she rolled over on her side and sank, more than 100 men trapped in her hull. Divers were down at once, but could do nothing to free the men.

Both men now stayed silent; the loss was horrible to consider. At last, speaking hoarsely, George said that there was little that he could do; but he should, he thought, at the very least show the solidarity of the Trust with the families who that day had lost their breadwinner and their family centre. As well he knew, the pattern on Clydeside was for as many able-bodied men as were in any one family to work together, and they were likely to be found in the same team. 'Please will you work on the ways in which we could institute a collection for the bereaved? We should try to extend our efforts beyond the generosity of the Trustees and make it as far as possible a public appeal. Meantime, please order me up a cab to Linthouse.'

Linthouse was downriver, and during the journey George had more than ample time to mashal his shocked reactions. Short on felicitous phrases in the circumstances, what, if any, could be the value of his simply being there, in the midst of bereavement? He thought of his wife Jean and what she would do. On arrival at Linthouse, the surging of the crowds and the lamentations of the people upset the horse pulling his cab. So he leaned out of the window and called out to the driver behind. 'Thank you; we cannot expect you to carry on any further. How much do I owe you?' The driver had difficulty working it out – he was as disconcerted as his horse. George climbed down, paid a generous amount, and thanked him for facing this journey, with its grim destination.

Then, watched still by the driver, George moved off to mingle with the distress on all sides. Ever recognizable, even by those who did not move in his circles, he was quickly surrounded by people who came up to grab his hand, some vaguely hoping, he realized, that he would, somehow, be able to work a magic of a kind and restore the ship to the surface. George knew that he must dispel thinking of this kind, without being harsh. The only solace must lie in facing up to reality. Then, feeling that what little he could do in the midst of the families was exhausted, he would try to find Alexander Stephen himself.

He was left in no doubt that this had been an appropriate move; the distressed shipbuilder even in his anguish was able to appreciate the Navigation Trust's identification with so savage a loss of both men and vessel. Even today, in many a Highland churchyard, you may find a headstone recalling the loss of those on board the *Daphne* that day.

Back at his desk, George was to encounter two matters which seemed to him to accord but poorly with the recent disaster. A letter awaited his attention from Lord Blantyre, a youthful landowner at East Ferry, whose interests included both the ferry at Erskine and the West Ferry on the north shore. The young lordship was withholding his permission for the building of any dykes and training walls within sight of his mansion, Erskine House. The letter seemed to George to be unnecessary as the Trustees had already conceded his point – namely that his view was spoiled – and so now relied on dredging only. This renewed complaint could hardly have come at a time better calculated to excite the disgust of the General Manager of the Navigation Trust, given the scene from which he had only just returned.

The second irritation for George that day was a Trustee writing in to propose as an agenda item a discussion on the feasibility of a modern, more prestigious building to house the headquarters of the Trust. In favour, argued the letter writer, was the enhanced standing and effectiveness of the Trust in the life of the city, and the high regard in which it was held, there and, indeed, nationally; the current office, though recently opened, gave the wrong impression. George wrote 'NO', initialled and dated it on the top corner of the sheet, and left Angus to take what, if any, action he thought necessary. At the next Board meeting the item, nevertheless, made its appearance on the agenda. George responded with irritated piety: that he, for one, had no interest whatsoever in vainglorious constructions; that if they insisted on following up this costly exercise in the face of the ways in which the money could be better spent many times over for the good of the enterprise, they must understand it would be without his concurrence. The second stage of the building's development was dropped for as long as George was in post, the proposer consuming his fire for some years, but springing into action soon after George had retired.

Since this man did, however, eventually get his way, today one of the most conspicuous buildings on the Broomielaw rose up in place of the tired premises preceding it. It was the work of the architect of the day, Sir J. J. Burnet, who received his commissions from all who wished to impress their publics. His domed building commands the corner; its excitable façade is crowded with antiquity's gods of the sea, along with their attendant sea-horses. Improbably they are seen to be hob-nobbing with lesser gods, nearer to our day: the giants of engineering and shipbuilding who made the Clyde and its noble products the matter of our continuing celebration – men such as John Golborne, James Watt, Thomas Telford, the Napier cousins and many more. Following this initial architectural exuberance, the building tapers away at its easterly corner: the First World War consumed the funds that were needed for its completion.

Burnet's building looked across to plenty of shipping on the south bank, all in such cheerful congestion as to make of their masts misty thickets, coming together like a smoke haze at the river's bend at Whiteinch. Near at hand were the quaintly tall, narrow little smoke stacks of busy coasters fussing about, above which rose the slender rigging of schooners whose masts, in all their delicacy, pricked the sky with tall grace. Giant cranes, George Reith's pride, like creatures of pre-history, were holding up the sky on their heads. The crane at Princes Dock weighed 130 tons and was steam driven; its purpose the fitting-out of vessels with their engines and boilers. It and its like had been ordered by the Trust, most particularly for shipyards without their own fitting-out basins. The backdrop to these scenes was the ceaseless din of chains dragged, rivets hammered, ships' sirens making their insistent assertions, and shunting engines hard at work shifting wagons.

Reith did not protest quite so loudly about the arrival one morning, of a gadget on his desk, whose purpose he could in no way fathom. Across its breadth it had a handle of sorts: he lifted it up, only to find that he had generated an energetic buzzing. As though in response, in came Angus Turner, noting that Mr Reith had been trying out his new telephone, and that his entry at this point demonstrated its purpose.

Understandably mystified still, George pointed out that he had found the bell that he pressed on his desk wholly satisfactory in making contact when he needed to. But when Angus pointed out the additional virtues of this new device George showed signs of interest, and went no further in dismissing it.

'How many people have these things now?' he wanted to know.

He learned that, since they had only come into use for the first time in 1879, four years ago, there were not many as yet. But, argued Angus, it would have become a disadvantage for the Trust to be in this way ill equipped.

George had no more objections to make, but humbly accepted the progress of technology.

Extraordinary, murmured Angus to his team in the office, that someone so ahead of the game as Mr Reith in engineering should be so uncertain about the work of Alexander Graham Bell and his telephones.

Mr Reith did view with the greatest displeasure, however, very many column inches of newsprint in the *Glasgow Herald* devoted to his fierce argument with one Nathaniel Dunlop, a Trustee. The issue was the collection of dues which Dunlop alleged were being demanded from each ship owner, although they should only be payable by the owners of the cargo – this being applicable to all shipping berthing in the port. In his charge he imputed that Reith had devised a system of charging from which, he inferred, Reith himself might profit.

Mr G.W. Clark, a fellow Trustee, spoke up at a Board meeting in such a way as to conclude the matter with some finality: 'I have known Mr Reith for upward of forty years, and a more noble, straightforward, and impartial man I never met. I believe Mr Reith is utterly incapable of doing the things which have been laid to his charge. It is impossible, I think, that Mr Reith could, from the very nature of the man, be swept aside a single bit from the path of rectitude and justice towards all men.' ('Hear, hear.') Reith's passionate supporter had more to say about the virtues of their General Manager, so much so that the matter was dismissed in Reith's favour, with further affirmations made on his many virtues. The Lord Provost concluded the meeting with an expression of his satisfaction at the outcome.

This was reported at baffling length in the *Glasgow Herald* of 19 October 1887. Reith laboured on in post for another two years; he was then persuaded by Jean to retire. She was worried that the stress of George's job was beginning to affect his health – not surprisingly, given that he had scarcely ever taken a holiday. One of her principal concerns was the continuing annoyance from the twelfth Lord Blantyre. Jean felt strongly that her husband was far too senior and experienced to have to endure the vexation of a self-centred aristocrat on the recurring theme of his spoiled view across the river, on account of training walls, dykes, buoys and so on. It was unfortunate that his lordship's approval was again needed for the Trustees to be able to carry out the river management that was essential to its overall navigability.

The next complaint centred on the claim that the policies of the Trust were causing the erosion of the Erskine foreshore. The case for no more dredging was taken to the House of Lords, where it was defeated. The Trustees were then sued for £100,000 for the damage done to the foreshore and lands, on account of an exceptionally high tide which brought up evil-smelling mud. The Court of Session ruled in favour of a claim on the Trustees of £12,500. They did, however, purchase all rights for the Erskine and the West Ferries.

If George was relieved at last to be out of range of the aggravation caused by Lord Blantyre, he now, as is the experience of many who have worked devotedly for many years, found that retirement presented him with its own challenges. But there were still advances and developments in Glasgow which interested and stimulated him. Jean said that they should go to see a series of murals, commissioned for the municipal banqueting hall in the imposing new City Chambers going up in George Square. They were to be executed by four of the leading 'Glasgow School' of artists. George Reith was moved by the wall panel by Sir John Lavery of 'Shipyard on the Clyde', catching, as it did with uncanny vigour, the din and clamour of it all.

George, with Jean's gentle encouragement, also took an interest in the building of the Kelvingrove Museum and Art Gallery on the banks of the River Kelvin. George was never to see this adventurous building (completed 1901), the work of a London firm of architects, Simpson and Allen. Their building materials were red Dumfries sandstone and the blue-green of the Westmorland slate for an exuberance of towers, minarets, rampant obelisks and so on which were to animate the roof-line. Jean felt sure that George's contribution to Glasgow and the west would figure in the midst of the exhibits within, and she told George so.

George was pleased; retirement had reduced his world, and he welcomed another event of a very different sort. He found himself peering into the cot of a very small baby boy, the seventh child of his younger son, George, and his wife Adah. The infant was to be named John, they said. George and his grandson had only a few months in which occasionally to meet.

Both grandfather and grandson, in his time, were achievers, each believing completely in the enterprise which he headed up, whether it was the Clyde or the BBC. A sketch of his grandfather always hung on a wall of John's office, whether in the BBC or elsewhere. The style developed by John was that of an impersonation of his grandfather, that Victorian patriarch, as he imagined him to be. John, finding it difficult to be a modern man – and particularly hard to admire a real figure of his day – was comfortable with his grandfather as role model. Family members recognized the many traits in his grandfather's character that recalled his own: both were autocratic, forbidding and unusually tall. Anyone they considered slow or inefficient got short shrift – their own managerial style, however, could never be questioned.

For George Reith, as was common with many of the great Victorian pioneers, it seems to have been a matter of personal commitment and inwardness expressed in a high moral tone, backed also, by an austere demeanour and severe management style. No wonder he was written up in *Fairplay* of December 1886 as being 'feared rather than loved by those he commands, but not the less is he held in high and general respect. He has been a good manager, although now somewhat old fashioned, decidedly obstinate and a trifle dreich.'

His own family may have found life with George oppressive. But his grandson John, brought up in the otherworldliness of a Free Church manse in Glasgow, made of religion a powerful instrument in his own battle for self-assertion. Through it he claimed to have been designated by the Almighty to carry out some great task for the nation, divine intervention assuring its achievement. Like his grandfather he became a melancholy religionist and a severe moralist.

To later generations, it may seem ironic that the dock had in modern times to suffer much of its area to be concreted over and on its massive foundations bear the weight of the audacity of the glass and steel cuboid building of his grandson's initiative: BBC Scotland. This was perhaps the material expression of the inheritance by one generation from that preceding; and with it the struggle by the one for supremacy over the other. George Reith was the man whose pioneering mission to open up the Clyde to navigation, shipbuilding and commerce was the inspiration and source of that force with which John Reith unlocked the BBC to its foundations of education, information and entertainment.

George retired at the end of October 1889. He thought with pride of the colossal initiative which would be the river's new Princes Dock, not yet built, but due to rise out of the old Cessnock Dock on the south bank over the coming years. He had been suffering from congestion and this was to become, as his obituary in 1889 explained, an effusion of blood to the brain. He died in his seventy-ninth year. Even if he would disclaim his achievements, his wife learned of the universal esteem in which he was held by successive Boards of Trustees.

In his early days in the job, when Reith first encountered the river in its deplorable state carrying untreated sewage, he had faced up to his Trustees with their entrenched view that the cleansing of the river was outwith their remit. Not long afterwards Reith was to be found seated alone on one side of a long table in the City Chambers, while opposite him was arranged a group of 12 from the City, finding their well-prepared arguments in favour of postponing the question of the treatment of raw sewage now dwindling into pale statements of little account. The health of thousands was at stake.

Much of George Reith's work on the Clyde has been swept away in the march of progress. The remnants of great docks, the wharves and their attendant facilities, and the 40 or so shipbuilding yards are scarcely traceable. But the story of the men of the river, with whom George Reith was proud to associate himself, and of the industrial revolution in Glasgow, much of which he inspired, lives on.

Epilogue

I was invited by my friend and publisher to write the story of my great-grandfather, George Reith.

He was General Manager of the Clyde Navigation Trust in the second half of the nineteenth century. I researched and found out a great deal about George Reith but there are, of course, inevitable gaps in the documentation available from the time. In order to give a more rounded account, I agreed with my publisher that it would take the form of a fictionalized history, that happy mode in which, as Rosemary Goring of the (Glasgow) *Herald* wrote 'history is given back its stories'.

And so, while the young George did, indeed, negotiate some days off from his Uncle John's wood yard, where he worked as a wheelwright, he was appropriately dissatisfied with his lowly job. He might find new openings through his young brother David, an advocate in Aberdeen.

All the evidence suggests that George would have been influenced and inspired by some of the great figures of his time. To convey that, in my fictionalized account George met up with Thomas Telford, with whom he fell into conversation. Telford was one of the greatest civil engineers ever! From their exchanges, there emerged George's stirrings to achieve, mingled with all the uncertainties and embarrassments of youth. Without such an invented scene, bold statements of fact lose the possibility of shades of meaning, calling for the reader's interpretation and giving, as a result, heightened interest.

The value of this mode has led to more fictionalized scenes, about each of which I have had to submit to the disciplines, attaching to the demands of clarification and relevance. These are also influenced by an understanding of George's character and approach to life – a family trait. Thus, I describe George's visit to Govan Old Parish Church, in which works Tommy; the hospitality of Robert Napier and his wife; the listening to a lecture by Lord Kelvin; the account of the launching of the *Queen Mary* by a former accountant at John Brown's yard – all these are invented scenes with which to animate the essential message.

On the other hand, many verifiable facts play their important part – the argument with the railway company over land at Stobcross also required by the Navigation Trust; the Atlantic crossing by Dickens on *Britannia*; the patient wait by Robert Napier to be recognized as the UK's most eminent ship builder of the day by the Admiralty – and so on.

Lastly, it would have been out of character had George Reith not used all his powers of persuasion on the state of the river into which was pumped untreated sewage. It would have been he who would have persuaded his own Trustees, and then the City corporation to act, so that the first treatment plant was eventually installed at Dalmarnock.

In essence, this is the story of a remarkable man who made a significant impact and I hope that the reader will derive the same enjoyment from reading this book as I did from researching it.

Marista Leishman